THE
INSIDER'S
SAT II
U.S. HISTORY
EXAM

THE ESSENTIAL CONTENT

LARRY KRIEGER
AND
JAN ALTMAN

The Insider's
SAT II U.S. History Exam:
The Essential Content

LARRY KRIEGER
and
JAN ALTMAN

ISBN: 978-0-9852912-3-5

An INSIDER TEST PREP publication of Larry Prep LLC

Art Direction & Design by
Station16 (Station16.com)

For more Insider resources visit
www.InsiderTestPrep.com

CONTENTS

PART 1

INTRODUCTION

ABOUT LARRY KRIEGER

Larry Krieger was born and raised in western North Carolina. He earned his Bachelor of Arts and Master of Arts in Teaching from the University of North Carolina at Chapel Hill and his Masters of Arts degree in Sociology from Wake Forest.

Larry's teaching career began in 1970 at Olympic High School in Charlotte, North Carolina. During the next 35 years Larry taught urban, rural, and suburban students in North Carolina and New Jersey. Larry taught a variety of AP and regular subjects including American History, World History, European History, American Government, Art History, Modern American History, and Sociology. His popular courses were renowned for their energetic presentations, commitment to scholarship, and dedication to excellence. All of Larry's students scored above a 700 on the SAT II U.S. History subject test and above a 3 on the AP U.S. History exam. In 2004 and 2005, the College Board recognized Larry as one of the nation's foremost AP teachers.

Larry's success has extended far beyond the classroom. He is the author of widely known Sociology, American History, and World History textbooks and a number of AP and SAT prep books. Larry founded InsiderTestPrep.com to share his AP, SAT II, and SAT I materials with students around the world. *The Insider's Essential Guide to the SAT II U.S. History Test* joins *The Insider's Essential Guide to the AP U.S. History Exam, SAT Critical Reading and Vocabulary and SAT Vocabulary: The Essential 500 Words* as the company's fourth major book. Insider Test Prep expects to publish a series of innovative SAT I, SAT II, and AP books in the near future.

ABOUT JAN ALTMAN

Jan Altman was born and raised in Dallas, Texas. She earned her Bachelor of Arts degree Cum Laude from Vanderbilt University. Jan currently lives in Louisville, Kentucky, and is very active in state and local organizations. For example, Jan served on the Board of Directors for the Learning Disabilities Association of Kentucky. She has also served in numerous extracurricular groups at Kentucky Country Day School and the Louisville Collegiate School.

Jan is now devoting a great deal of time and energy to preparing students for the ACT, SAT I, SAT II U.S. History test, and AP U.S. History exams. Jan is an indefatigable researcher who has created unique review materials that have helped her students achieve exemplary test scores.

ACKNOWLEDGMENTS

Books do not write themselves. They require the help of a number of dedicated and creative people.

First and foremost, Jan and I would like to thank our spouses Billy and Susan. Every chapter benefited from their "close reads" and advice.

We would also like to thank our students. Both Jan and I have been blessed with an exceptional number of outstanding students. Each of the students named in our Board of Student Advisors contributed suggestions that have been incorporated into our book.

BOARD OF STUDENT ADVISORS

PROLOGUE

I. BASIC FEATURES OF THE SAT II U.S. HISTORY TEST

QUESTIONS

1. The SAT II U.S. History test consists of 90 multiple-choice questions. You are given 60 minutes to answer these questions.

2. The 90 multiple-choice questions are distributed into the following three broad chronological periods:
   - Pre-Columbian to 1789   20% or 18 questions
   - 1790–1898   40% or 36 questions
   - 1899–Present   40% or 36 questions

3. The SAT II U.S. History test typically contains one or two questions on topics before the founding of Jamestown in 1607 and three or four questions about important events and demographic trends since the inauguration of President Reagan in 1981.

4. The 90 multiple-choice questions are distributed into the following five broad thematic areas:
   - Political history   31–35 percent
   - Economic history   13–17 percent
   - Social history   20–24 percent
   - Intellectual and cultural history 13–17 percent
   - Foreign policy   13–17 percent

SCORING

5. Each multiple-choice question is worth one point. So 90 is a perfect score.

6. The College Board still subtracts 0.25 points for each wrong answer. For example, if you correctly answer 66 questions and miss 24, your raw score will be 66 minus 6, or 60. No points are awarded for unanswered questions.

7. *The College Board's Official Study Guide for all SAT Subject Tests* includes a sample U.S. History test. The scale on page 91 indicates that a raw score of 79 to 90 will translate into an 800. Here are several benchmark scores from this scale:

Raw Score	Scaled Score
90	800
85	800
80	800
75	770
70	730
65	700
60	670
55	650
50	620
45	600
40	570
35	540
30	520
25	490
20	460
15	440
10	410
5	390

This scale appears to be very generous. It is important to point out that many students are now reporting that recent tests use a much harsher scale

II. RETHINKING HOW TO PREPARE FOR THE SAT II U.S. HISTORY TEST

THE TRADITIONAL APPROACH

8. The College Board recommends that you prepare for the SAT II U.S. History test by taking a challenging class, studying hard, and learning as much of the classroom material as possible. This "classroom material" often includes long review packets that contain hundreds of unrelated pieces of information.

A NEW LOOK AT THE TRADITIONAL APPROACH

9. The traditional approach assumes that the best way to prepare for the SAT II U.S. History test is to master the content in your textbook by studying literally everything. Is this really the most effective way to prepare for this test?

10. Take another look at the SAT II U.S. History scale on page IX. It is important to note that you can earn an 800 by correctly answering 80 or 88.8 percent of the 90 questions. You can earn a 700 by correctly answering just 72.2 percent of the questions!

11. This analysis convincingly reveals that you do NOT need to master your entire textbook to achieve a high score. But if you don't study everything, what should you study? An exhaustive analysis of SAT II U.S. History tests reveals that the questions cluster around a predictable group of key topics. This discovery makes your job of preparing for the SAT II U.S. History test much easier!

III. A BOLD NEW BOOK

A NEW SELECTIVE APPROACH

12. The traditional approach of preparing for the SAT II U.S. History test by studying an exhaustive list of historic information is clearly inefficient and unnecessary.

13. Insider Test Prep advocates a new, selective approach that incorporates the following two principles:
    - Ignore topics that rarely if ever generate questions.
    - Focus on topical clusters that generate the overwhelming majority of questions.

UNIQUE FEATURES OF THE ESSENTIAL GUIDE TO THE SAT II U.S. HISTORY TEST:

UNIQUE NARRATIVE REVIEW

14. Narrative Review
    - Essential opens with a 34-chapter narrative review that begins with a chapter on "Pre-Columbian America" and concludes with a chapter on "Key Events and Trends, 1980–Present." These chapters are designed to provide you with succinct summaries that will enable you to understand the historic context of key events, trends, and quotes.
    - Each chapter is built around topics and key points that College Board test writers repeatedly test. There is thus a direct correlation between the space we devote to a topic and its importance on the test. If we omit a topic, it is because it has not generated any test questions.

UNIQUE SUPER FAST REVIEW

15. Super Fast Review
    - Students preparing for the SAT II U.S. History test must also prepare for the SAT I, ACT, AP exams, and of course school assignments and tests.
    - Our Super Fast Review is designed to live up to its title! It is a carefully organized statement of the key facts, terms, and events you absolutely, positively have to know to achieve a high score on your SAT II U.S. History test.

UNIQUE COLLECTION OF QUOTES

16. Quotes

- SAT II U.S. History tests typically devote eight to ten questions to historic quotes. These quote-questions test your knowledge of key concepts, events, and trends. Many students find these quote-based questions the most challenging questions on the test.
- Essential provides you with a chronological list of 70 key quotes. We introduce each of these quotes with a succinct statement that tells you why the quote is important.

UNIQUE COLLECTION OF LISTS

17. Lists

- College Board test writers expect you to know a core group of key people, presidents, elections, amendments, and acts of Congress. These items typically generate a significant number of test questions.
- Essential provides you with carefully organized lists of key people, events, and laws that have generated a significant number of test questions. These lists will enable you to efficiently review this key historic information.

UNIQUE PRACTICE TEST

18. PRACTICE TEST

- The College Board has provided students with just two practice tests.
- Essential provides you with a practice test that is designed to be a close replica of an actual SAT II U.S. History test.

GOOD LUCK!

Jan and I have taught U.S. History students for a combined total of over 40 years! Essential contains a lifetime of key points, strategies, and tips. Almost all of our students have scored above a 700 on the SAT II U.S. History test. You will too!

—PART 1—
NARRATIVE REVIEW

CHAPTER 1
PRE-COLUMBIAN AMERICA

A. THE FIRST AMERICANS

1. Most experts agree that hunters from Asia inadvertently discovered the Americas some 30,000 to 40,000 years ago.
2. According to a widely accepted hypothesis, the hunters probably crossed a natural land bridge stretching from eastern Siberia to Alaska.

B. CHARACTERISTIC FEATURES OF PRE-COLUMBIAN NATIVE PEOPLES

1. Pre-Columbian Native Peoples developed a mathematically based calendar, constructed irrigation systems, built multi-family dwellings, lived in cities inhabited by 100,000 or more people, practiced a division of labor based upon gender, and cultivated maize (also known as Indian corn).
2. Pre-Columbian Native Peoples did NOT develop wheeled vehicles, water wheels, or have tribal property rights.

C. NATIVE PEOPLES IN NORTH AMERICA

1. People in the Pacific Northwest relied on hunting and fishing for food.
2. The Anasazis of the Southwest were a sedentary, agricultural people who built elaborate pueblos.
3. Eastern Woodland people lived in village communities and had agricultural economies based on the cultivation of maize. Political and linguistic differences made it difficult for Eastern Woodland tribes to form alliances to oppose the European colonists and trappers.

4. Many of the Eastern Woodland tribes lived in matrilineal societies in which inheritance passed through the mother's clan.

5. Unlike the other Eastern Woodland tribes, the Iroquois successfully formed a powerful political alliance known as the Iroquois Confederacy. The alliance ended generations of warfare and formed the most important North American organization to confront the colonists.

6. The Iroquois lived in permanent settlements. (It is interesting to note that, in contrast, the Sioux were nomadic.)

7. The Creeks, Cherokee, and Chickasaw were all Native American tribes living in the Eastern Woodlands.

8. Women were the primary farmers among the Eastern Woodland tribes. In contrast, men were the primary farmers among the English colonists.

CHAPTER 2
NEW SPAIN AND NEW FRANCE

A. PORTUGAL
1. Portugal was the first country to conduct regular maritime expeditions in the South Atlantic.
2. The Portuguese explored the west coast of Africa and also discovered Brazil.
3. The Portuguese began the Atlantic slave trade.

B. CHRISTOPHER COLUMBUS
1. Spain was the first European nation to systematically explore the New World.
2. Columbus actually intended to find a new and shorter route to Asia.

C. THE CONQUISTADORES
1. Hernán Cortés conquered the Aztecs.
2. Francisco Pizarro conquered the Incas.
3. Both Cortés and Pizarro defeated and overthrew rulers who led centralized governments.
4. European diseases such as smallpox aided the Spanish conquest by decimating the populations of New World peoples.

D. THE COLUMBIAN EXCHANGE
1. The Spanish began the COLUMBIAN EXCHANGE.
2. The Columbian Exchange refers to the exchange of plants, animals, and diseases between Europe and the New World.
3. For example, maize, potatoes, and tomatoes were all New World crops that revolutionized the European diet. Horses, cows, and pigs were all domesticated European animals that revolutionized life in the New World.

E. CHARACTERISTIC FEATURES OF NEW SPAIN

1. The Spanish established a New World empire in order to convert the native population to Christianity and enhance Spanish prestige by achieving greater wealth and power.
2. Spain created a bureaucratic New World government that was largely controlled from Madrid. It is important to note that Spanish bureaucrats were NOT recruited from Native American groups.
3. The Catholic Church sent missionaries to convert native populations to Christianity.
4. A majority of the early Spanish colonists were single men who did NOT expect to settle in the New World.
5. The Spanish found and exploited rich silver mines in Mexico and Peru.

F. FLORIDA

1. The Spanish discovered and colonized Florida.
2. Florida was the first part of what is now the United States to be settled by Europeans.
3. St. Augustine was the first permanent settlement in what is today the United States.

G. THE SPANISH SOUTHWEST

1. The Spanish gradually gained control over New Mexico and the Pueblo.
2. In 1680, a charismatic Pueblo leader named Popé organized a widespread rebellion known as the Pueblo Revolt.
3. The Pueblo Revolt succeeded in driving the Spanish out of the upper Rio Grande region for nearly a decade. However, Popé died in 1688, robbing the Pueblo of their inspirational leader and enabling the Spanish to begin a gradual reconquest of the region.
4. The Spanish also had extensive contact with the Hopi and the Zuni.

H. NEW FRANCE

1. The French explored the Great Lakes and the Mississippi River Valley.

2. French fur traders and trappers dominated the lucrative fur trade. Beaver skins were France's major "money crop." In the best years, traders bought and sold over 100,000 beaver skins. In 1693, a fleet of 400 Indian canoes brought furs to Montreal.

3. The French fur traders developed a cooperative relationship with the Native American tribes. Unlike the English settlers, they did not build plantations and farms on lands claimed by Native Americans.

CHAPTER 3
VIRGINIA AND THE SOUTHERN COLONIES

A. SIR WALTER RALEIGH AND ROANOKE

1. Sir Walter Raleigh attempted to found a colony on Roanoke Island, off the coast of present-day North Carolina. The colony failed, however, and the fate of the colonists is still a mystery.
2. The failure of the Roanoke colony prompted English investors to form JOINT-STOCK COMPANIES to finance colonization projects in North America. A joint-stock company is a financial arrangement, in which investors share the risks and profits in proportion to their portion of the total investment.

B. JAMESTOWN AND EARLY VIRGINIA

1. Jamestown was founded by the Virginia Company, a joint-stock company dedicated to making a profit.
2. Jamestown and the Virginia colony were NOT founded to promote religious toleration.
3. The early Jamestown settlers encountered a Native American alliance known as the Powhatan Confederacy.
4. Virginia was the first colony to cultivate tobacco as a cash crop. The improved type of tobacco developed by John Rolfe saved the Virginia colony from financial ruin.
5. Virginia's House of Burgesses was the first example of a representative assembly in Britain's North American colonies.
6. The early Virginia colony had far more men than women. The scarcity of women strengthened the socioeconomic status of women relative to women in England.
7. The Virginia colony lost its charter in 1624, and Virginia became the first royal colony.

C. EARLY MARYLAND

1. Lord Baltimore founded Maryland as a religious refuge for Roman Catholics.
2. The Maryland Act of Religious Toleration protected Catholics from religious persecution by Protestants.
3. Maryland and Virginia are known as the Chesapeake colonies.

D. INDENTURED SERVANTS

1. The cultivation of tobacco required a large labor force.
2. Indentured servants were English men and women who agreed to work for a master for a term of four to seven years. In return, the master paid their way to Virginia and gave them food, clothing, and shelter.
3. The labor of indentured servants was an essential factor in the growth of the early plantation system.
4. The HEADRIGHT SYSTEM promoted the use of indentured servants. Virginia planters received 50 acres for each person (or head) they brought to the colony. Indentured servants comprised the largest portion of Virginia's labor force prior to 1675.
5. The labor of indentured servants could not be bought, sold, or willed. Indentured servants could not marry without the permission of their master. However, indentured servants could be taught to read and write.

E. BACON'S REBELLION

1. Discontented frontier farmers, many of whom had been indentured servants, rebelled against the arbitrary rule of Governor Berkeley and the haughty class of wealthy planters he represented.
2. Led by Nathaniel Bacon, the rebels captured and burned down Jamestown. But Bacon's sudden death from dysentery enabled Berkeley to regain the upper hand and crush the rebellion.
3. Bacon's Rebellion was the largest rebellion in the colonial period. It exposed the tensions between the wealthy planters and the poor former indentured servants.
4. Bacon's Rebellion encouraged Chesapeake planters to replace difficult-to-control indentured servants with black slaves imported from Africa.

F. THE GROWTH OF SLAVERY

1. The supply of potential indentured servants began to dwindle as economic conditions in England improved.
2. The profitable cultivation of tobacco required inexpensive labor. Slavery grew rapidly in the late 17th century as blacks replaced indentured servants in the Virginia and Maryland tobacco plantations.
3. England wanted a share of the profitable tobacco trade begun by the Portuguese and continued by the Dutch.
4. It is important to remember that the vast majority of African slaves who survived the transatlantic voyage to the New World worked on sugar plantations in Brazil and the Caribbean islands.

G. SOUTH CAROLINA

1. Rice was South Carolina's most important cash crop in the mid-18th century.
2. South Carolina planters also grew indigo. It is important to note that indigo was much less labor-intensive than either tobacco or rice.

H. GEORGIA

1. Georgia was founded in 1733 to create a buffer between South Carolina and Spanish Florida.
2. Georgia was the last of Great Britain's thirteen North American colonies.

CHAPTER 4
THE PURITANS AND THE QUAKERS

A. THE PILGRIMS

1. The Pilgrims were Separatists who wanted to sever all ties with the Church of England.
2. The Mayflower Compact was a solemn agreement, or covenant, to make political decisions based upon the will of the people.

B. THE PURITANS

1. The Puritans wanted to remove or purify the elaborate rituals and decorative ornaments used by the Church of England.
2. John Winthrop defined the purpose of the Puritan mission in a sermon delivered onboard the flagship *Arabella*.
3. QUOTE: "For we must consider that we shall be as a city upon a hill, the eyes of all people are upon us. So that if we shall deal falsely with our God in this work we shall have undertaken, and so cause Him to withdraw His present help from us, we shall be made a story and a by-word through the world." John Winthrop
4. John Winthrop expressed the Puritan belief that they had a special pact with God to build a model Christian society.
5. It is interesting to note that the Puritans actually landed off course. As a result, they were transformed from a joint-stock company into a self-governing colony.

C. KEY CHARACTERISTICS OF PURITAN SOCIETY

1. The Puritans migrated to New England in family groups rather than as single individuals.
2. The Puritans believed that a model community required a close relationship between church and state.

3. A strict code of moral conduct guided Puritan society. Puritans believed in the moral authority of the community over individual self-interest.
4. Puritans typically lived in compact villages clustered around a church or meeting house.
5. The Puritans valued education as a means to enable people to read and understand the Bible. They required each community of 50 or more families to provide a teacher of reading and writing. The Puritans founded Harvard College to train ministers.
6. The Puritans did NOT believe in the innate goodness of human nature.
7. The Puritans did NOT cultivate cash crops, encourage women to take leadership roles, maintain peaceful relations with local Native American tribes, or suppress slave revolts.

D. RELIGIOUS DISSENTERS

1. Although the Puritans came to America for religious freedom, they did NOT tolerate outspoken religious dissenters.
2. The Puritans banished Anne Hutchinson because of her unorthodox religious views. Hutchinson challenged the clergy's ability to interpret the Bible and also claimed to have had a revelation from God.
3. The Puritans banished Roger Williams for his unorthodox religious and political views. Williams championed the cause of religious toleration and freedom of thought. He advocated the separation of church and state, arguing that the state was an inappropriate organization to interfere in matters of faith.

E. THE HALFWAY COVENANT

1. By the late 1600s, women were rapidly becoming a majority in many church congregations.
2. The HALFWAY COVENANT was a response to the decline of religious zeal among the Puritans.
3. The Halfway Covenant relaxed the requirements for church membership.

F. SEEDS OF COLONIAL UNITY

1. The New England Confederation marked an early attempt to coordinate the defense of frontier settlements from threats by the Indians and the French.
2. Unlike the homegrown New England Confederation, the Dominion of New England was created by the royal authorities in London. The Dominion of New England collapsed following the 1688 Glorious Revolution in England.

G. THE QUAKERS

1. Quakers were a group of religious dissenters who appeared in England in the mid-1600s.
2. Quakers believed that every person had an inner light and needed only to live by it to be saved. Since every person has an inner light, all people are equal.
3. The Quakers were pacifists who refused to bear arms. They advocated religious toleration, opposed slavery, and allowed women to speak publicly in religious meetings.
4. Quakers did NOT refuse to pay taxes or practice clerical celibacy.

H. WILLIAM PENN AND PENNSYLVANIA

1. William Penn founded Pennsylvania as a "Holy Experiment" that would serve as a refuge for Quakers.
2. Penn launched an aggressive campaign to encourage people to settle in his colony. As a result, Pennsylvania attracted a diverse mix of ethnic groups.
3. Pennsylvania had an assembly elected by landowners.
4. Pennsylvania did NOT have an established church or hostile relations with the local Indian tribes.

CHAPTER 5
LIFE AND THOUGHT IN COLONIAL AMERICA

A. THE FIRST GREAT AWAKENING

1. The FIRST GREAT AWAKENING was a wave of religious revivals that began in New England in the mid-1730s and swept across the colonies during the 1740s.
2. "New Light" ministers such as Jonathan Edwards and George Whitefield deemphasized ceremony and ritual. Instead, they advocated an emotional approach to religious practice that threatened the authority of the "Old Light" Puritan ministers.
3. The First Great Awakening promoted the growth of institutions of higher learning by leading to the founding of "New Light" colleges such as Princeton, Rutgers, and Dartmouth.
4. The First Great Awakening weakened the authority of "Old Light" Puritan ministers, split the Presbyterian and Congregational churches, involved more women in church congregations, and brought Christianity to the African slaves.
5. The Great Awakening increased the number of Protestant sects, thus promoting religious pluralism and toleration, since no single denomination could impose its dogma on the others.
6. The First Great Awakening did NOT lead to legislative efforts to emancipate the slaves.

B. MERCANTILISM

1. MERCANTILISM was a British economic policy designed to achieve a favorable balance of trade by exporting more goods than it imported. In order to achieve this goal, Great Britain purchased raw materials from its American colonies and then sold them more expensive manufactured goods.

2. Mercantilism was designed to protect British industries and make the colonies dependent upon their mother country.
3. The Navigation Acts implemented Britain's mercantilist policies. For example, specific acts limited the export of tobacco, indigo, beaver pelts, and other enumerated goods to only English ships.
4. Colonial cities such as Boston, New York, and Philadelphia functioned primarily as mercantile centers that maintained close economic ties with Great Britain. It is important to note that although most colonial cities were located on rivers, they were NOT connected by a system of rivers.
5. The Navigation Acts were not rigorously enforced prior to 1763. During this period of "salutary neglect," enterprising colonial merchants successfully evaded burdensome mercantile regulations. For example, New England merchants profited greatly from illegally trading fish and lumber to French possessions in the Caribbean. As a result, the colonists developed a growing spirit of economic independence.

C. WOMEN IN COLONIAL AMERICA

1. A married woman had no separate legal identity apart from her husband.
2. Single women and widows had the legal right to own property. However, they could NOT hold political office, vote, or serve on juries.
3. Colonial women were often midwives.

D. AFRICAN AMERICANS IN COLONIAL AMERICA

1. The number of slaves increased rapidly in the last quarter of the 17th century and throughout the 18th century.
2. Although slavery was legal in all 13 colonies, about 90 percent of all slaves lived and worked in the South.
3. Slaves were able to maintain cultural practices brought from Africa.

E. THE ENLIGHTENMENT

1. DEISM was an important part of the Enlightenment. Deists believed that natural laws regulated both the universe and human society. These natural laws could be discovered by human reason. The discovery of natural laws of economics and government would improve society and make progress inevitable.
2. Ben Franklin was a renowned Deist whose varied achievements best exemplified the Enlightenment in British North America.
3. The influence of the Enlightenment can also be seen in the widespread belief that there are universal and inalienable natural rights that all governments must respect.

F. THE JOHN PETER ZENGER CASE

1. Zenger's newspaper sharply criticized New York's corrupt royal governor.
2. Zenger was charged with seditious libel.
3. The jury found Zenger not guilty. The verdict established the legal principle that true statements about public figures could not be prosecuted as libel.
4. The Zenger case sparked debate about freedom of the press. It is interesting to note that Sam Adams fought for the Zenger case and for freedom of the press.

CHAPTER 6
SEVERING TIES WITH GREAT BRITAIN, 1754-1783

A. THE ALBANY PLAN OF UNION, 1754

1. Inspired by Benjamin Franklin, the Albany Plan of Union was an attempt to achieve greater colonial unity by providing for the common defense against the French and Indian threats to frontier settlements.
2. The Albany Plan was not adopted because the colonies did NOT want to give up their autonomy.
3. Franklin's famous "Join, or Die" cartoon dramatically illustrated the pressing need for greater colonial unity.

4. Although the Albany Plan failed to unify the colonies, newspapers and pamphlets did encourage cross-colony unity before 1763.

B. THE FRENCH AND INDIAN WAR, 1754-1763

1. The Algonquian supported the French, and the Iroquois supported the English.
2. Led by William Pitt, England won the French and Indian War. England's large population of permanent settlers proved to be an overwhelming advantage.

3. The terms of the Peace of Paris forced France to relinquish almost all of its New World empire. England now controlled France's former Canadian territories and all lands east of the Mississippi River.

C. PONTIAC'S REBELLION, 1763

1. Pontiac was an Ottawa leader who formed a strong Indian alliance. In May 1763, these allied tribes began a war against the British that is known as Pontiac's Rebellion. (Needless to say, Pontiac's Rebellion was NOT a slave rebellion!)
2. Pontiac's men killed some 2,000 settlers and at one point captured eight of twelve British forts west of the Allegheny Mountains.
3. Despite these heavy losses, the British finally defeated Pontiac and ended the fighting.

D. THE PROCLAMATION LINE OF 1763

1. Pontiac's Rebellion prompted the British to issue the Proclamation Line of 1763.
2. In order to avoid further clashes with the trans-Appalachian Indians, the British forbade the colonists from crossing an imaginary boundary set at the crest of the Appalachian Mountains.
3. Many colonists resented the Proclamation Line. They soon defied it by pushing over the Appalachian ridges and crossing into Kentucky and Tennessee.

E. THE SUGAR ACT, 1764

1. The Sugar Act marked Parliament's first attempt to enforce the Navigation Acts, thus ending the period of salutary neglect.
2. Under the terms of the Sugar Act, smugglers could be tried without a jury in the new admiralty courts in Halifax, Nova Scotia.

F. THE STAMP ACT, 1765

1. The French and Indian War doubled Britain's national debt. Indignant royal officials pointed out that the average person in Great Britain had a debt 45 times as great as that of the average colonist.

2. Parliament passed the Stamp Act to raise revenue to help pay for British troops stationed in America.
3. The Stamp Act provoked a contentious debate over Parliament's constitutional right to tax its American colonies.
4. British leaders argued that Parliament was based upon a system of VIRTUAL REPRESENTATION, in which each member of Parliament represented the interests of all Englishmen, including the colonists.
5. The colonists rejected virtual representation, arguing that as Englishmen they could only be taxed by their own elected representatives.
6. The Stamp Act Congress called for a boycott of British goods. The boycott proved to be an effective way to influence Parliament. Pressured by angry British exporters, Parliament agreed to repeal the Stamp Act.
7. However, Parliament also passed a Declaratory Act adamantly insisting on its right to tax the colonies.

G. REPUBLICANISM

1. REPUBLICANISM is the belief that government should be based on the consent of the governed. It is important to note that the colonists had a long-standing tradition of making local decisions in town meetings.
2. The Stamp Act crisis intensified the colonial commitment to republican values. The colonists strongly believed that in a representative government, sovereignty is located in the people.
3. Key republican values included a fear of standing armies, a belief in the virtue of agrarian life, and a firm commitment to rule by locally elected representatives.

H. THE BOSTON MASSACRE, 1770

1. On the night of March 5, 1770, a rowdy group of hecklers taunted a squad of British soldiers outside the Boston Customs house. A soldier fired into the crowd, and when the smoke cleared, five townspeople lay on the ground, dead or dying.

2. Led by Sam Adams, enraged patriots promptly branded the incident the "Boston Massacre." Paul Revere's highly partisan engraving further inflamed colonial opinion by depicting the British soldiers as merciless brutes who killed innocent civilians.

I. THE INTOLERABLE ACTS

1. Parliament enacted the Intolerable (or Coercive Acts) to punish Boston for the losses to property caused by the Boston Tea Party.
2. The Intolerable Acts were designed to increase Parliament's control over the colonies in general and Boston in particular.
3. The Intolerable Acts led to the calling of the First Continental Congress.

J. *COMMON SENSE*, 1776

1. Although tensions between the colonies and the British government mounted, most colonists still did not want to completely cut all ties with their mother country.
2. Thomas Paine strongly disagreed with this loyalist sentiment. In January 1776 he published a pamphlet entitled *Common Sense* to persuade the colonists to declare their independence from Britain.
3. Paine vigorously defended republican principles while denouncing monarchy as a form of government that produced a constant threat to people's liberty. For example, he compared King George III to a callous pharaoh who had no sympathies for his subjects.
4. QUOTE: "But Britain is the parent country say some. Then more shame upon her conduct. Even brutes do not devour their young, nor savages make war upon their families...This new world has been the asylum for the persecuted lovers of civil and religious liberty from every part of Europe." Thomas Paine
5. Paine rejected calls for a compromise with England and instead urged Americans to declare their independence and start a new republic.
6. *Common Sense* reached a significant portion of the colonial population. It played a key role in persuading Americans to seek independence from Great Britain.

K. "REMEMBER THE LADIES"

1. Abigail Adams was a well-educated woman who was an early proponent of women's rights.
2. In a private letter written only three months before the writing of the Declaration of Independence, Abigail urged her husband John Adams to "remember the Ladies" as he and his fellow members of the Second Continental Congress debated America's future.
3. QUOTE: "In the new Code of Laws which I suppose it will be necessary for you to make, I desire you would remember the Ladies, and be more generous and favorable to them than your ancestors. Do not put such unlimited power into the hands of Husbands. Remember all Men would be tyrants if they could."
4. Abigail's famous request underscored the fact that colonial women were treated as second-class citizens. Her letter demonstrates that some colonial women were aware of the discrepancy between the republican ideal of equality and the reality of how women were treated.

L. THE DECLARATION OF INDEPENDENCE, 1776

1. Thomas Jefferson opened the Declaration of Independence with a list of inalienable rights that was influenced by John Locke's theory of natural rights.
2. Jefferson then appealed to the sympathies of fair-minded readers by listing a number of specific grievances against King George III. Taken together, these grievances demonstrated that George III was a tyrant who was guilty of "repeated injustices and usurpations."
3. The Declaration of Independence did NOT call for the abolition of the slave trade. It is important to note that Southern slave owners were NOT afraid that the British would ban slavery.
4. Kentucky, Maine, and Vermont did NOT sign the Declaration of Independence since they were not yet states.
5. Jefferson and the other signers believed that state governments were the real source of power in the colonies.

M. THE WAR FOR INDEPENDENCE, 1776-1783

1. The American victory at Saratoga marked a crucial turning point in the War for Independence. The victory prevented the British from isolating the New England colonies. It also persuaded the French to declare war on Great Britain and openly aid the American cause.
2. The French king Louis XVI did not support America because he was sympathetic to republican values. Instead, the French king was motivated by a desire to avenge his country's humiliating defeat in the French and Indian War.
3. The French alliance prevented any chance of an Anglo-American reconciliation. French naval power played a decisive role in enabling General George Washington to win the Battle of Yorktown and end the war.
4. Colonial leaders formed a Continental Army because the local militias proved to be unreliable.
5. The Continental Congress was NOT dominated by Tories loyal to Great Britain.
6. During the war, Native Americans allied with the British or the Americans depending upon their own self-interests.
7. A serious lack of funds hampered the colonial war effort. The depreciation of the government's paper currency led to unrest in the Continental Army.

N. THE TREATY OF PARIS

1. Great Britain recognized the independence of the United States.
2. The treaty recognized American sovereignty over territories extending from the Mississippi River on the west, to the Great Lakes on the north, and to Spanish Florida on the south.

CHAPTER 7
FORMING A NEW NATIONAL GOVERNMENT, 1781-1789

A. THE ARTICLES OF CONFEDERATION

1. The 13 original states ratified the Articles of Confederation in 1781. It is important to remember that most Americans favored a loose confederation of states with a limited central government. The Continental Congress was therefore careful to avoid giving the new Articles of Confederation powers it had just denied to Parliament.

2. The Articles of Confederation created a government consisting of only a unicameral legislature. The government did NOT have an executive or a judicial branch.

3. The Articles of Confederation created a "firm league of friendship" that could NOT exercise power independent of the states. For example, Congress could NOT tax the people, regulate trade, or raise an army. Congress could only ask the states for money and soldiers.

B. THE NORTHWEST ORDINANCE OF 1787

1. The region originally known as the Northwest Territory included lands north of the Ohio River, east of the Mississippi River, and south of the Great Lakes.

2. The Northwest Ordinance of 1787 provided an orderly procedure for territories to become new states on an equal basis with the original 13 states.

3. Ohio was the first state to enter the Union from the Northwest Territory.

4. The Northwest Ordinance was the first national law to ban slavery from a specific region.

5. The Northwest Ordinance did NOT provide free land for settlers or financial compensation for Native Americans.

C. PRESSING PROBLEMS

1. The Articles of Confederation faced a number of pressing problems. For example, the new nation lacked a uniform currency, faced unresolved border disputes between states, and confronted the continued presence of British soldiers on American soil.
2. The Articles of Confederation did NOT face a problem from Loyalists who refused to lay down their arms.

D. SHAYS' REBELLION

1. In the Fall of 1786, farmers in western Massachusetts were losing their farms because they could not repay their debts in hard currency to eastern merchants and bankers.
2. Led by Daniel Shays, the desperate farmers demanded that the Massachusetts legislature halt farm foreclosures, lower property taxes, print paper money, and end imprisonment for debt.
3. It is important to note that Shays and his followers did NOT try to overthrow the Massachusetts government or instigate a war against the Indians.
4. Although state troops quickly routed Shays' men, the rebellion frightened conservative leaders by exposing the inability of the Articles of Confederation to protect property. Key leaders such as James Madison, Alexander Hamilton, and George Washington called for a Constitutional Convention that would replace the Articles of Confederation with a stronger national government.

E. KEY PRINCIPLES UNDERLYING THE CONSTITUTION

1. The Constitution is built on a series of compromises.
2. The framers opposed political parties. They saw them as vehicles of ambition that would threaten the existence of representative government.
3. James Madison believed that a large republic would curb factionalism.
4. QUOTE: "In an expanding Republic, so many different groups and viewpoints would be included in the Congress that tyranny by the majority would be impossible." James Madison

5. The framers created a FEDERAL system of government in which a written constitution divides power between a central government and state governments.

F. THE GREAT COMPROMISE

1. The Great Compromise resolved a dispute between the large states, led by Virginia, and the small states, led by New Jersey.
2. The Great Compromise created a bicameral, or two-house, Congress. Representation in the House of Representatives would be apportioned on the basis of population, while each state would be allotted two seats in the Senate.

G. THE THREE-FIFTHS COMPROMISE

1. The words *slave* and *slavery* do NOT appear in the original Constitution. However, the framers did indirectly recognize slavery in the Three-Fifths Compromise.
2. The Three-Fifths Compromise resolved a dispute between the slave states and the free states. Under the terms of this compromise, each slave counted as three-fifths of a person for purposes of determining a state's level of taxation and representation. This increased the congressional representation of the slave states and also gave them a greater voice in the Electoral College.
3. It is important to note that the framers' decision to allow the importation of slaves to continue until 1808 also indirectly recognized the existence of slavery.

H. KEY PROVISIONS THAT WERE PART OF THE CONSTITUTION SUBMITTED TO THE STATES IN 1787

1. A bicameral Congress with the power to levy taxes, declare war, and regulate interstate commerce.
2. A separation of powers in which the government is divided into executive, legislative, and judicial branches.
3. A system of checks and balances among the three branches of government. Alexander Hamilton argued that the system of checks and balances would curtail abuses of power and thus protect liberty: "There is no liberty if the power to judge be not separated from the powers to make and carry out the laws."

4. An Electoral College designed to safeguard the presidency from direct popular election.

5. A "necessary and proper" clause, also known as the elastic clause, that gives Congress the power to make laws necessary for carrying out its enumerated powers. It is interesting to note that the necessary and proper clause contradicted many of the framers' commitment to states' rights.

6. A provision calling for an annual presidential State of the Union address.

7. A provision for impeaching the President.

I. KEY PROVISIONS THAT WERE NOT IN THE CONSTITUTION SUBMITTED TO THE STATES IN 1787

1. A Bill of Rights.
2. Political parties.
3. A two-term limit for the President.
4. Universal manhood suffrage.
5. A presidential cabinet.
6. The direct election of senators.
7. The President cannot appoint the Speaker of the House.
8. The right to a speedy and public trial.

J. THE ANTI-FEDERALISTS VERSUS THE FEDERALISTS

1. The Constitution did would NOT go into effect until it was ratified by at least nine of the 13 states.

2. A fierce battle erupted between Federalists, who supported the Constitution, and Anti-Federalists, who opposed it.

3. The Anti-Federalists drew their primary support from small farmers and rural areas. They argued that the proposed Constitution lacked a Bill of Rights and that the new national government would dominate the states and threaten individual liberties.

4. Patrick Henry opposed the new Constitution. In the ratification debate in Virginia, Henry asked: "Is this a confederacy, like Holland—an association of independent states, each of which retains its individual sovereignty?" Henry went on to declare: "It is not a democracy, wherein the people retain their rights securely. Had these principles been adhered to, we should not have been brought to this alarming transition from a confederation to a consolidated government." It is interesting to note that later states' rights leaders such as John C. Calhoun would approvingly use Henry's famous quote.

5. The Federalists drew their primary support from large landowners, wealthy merchants, and urban areas. They argued that the proposed Constitution would create a federal government with enough power to promote the general welfare and ensure domestic tranquility by quickly responding to disturbances such as Shays' Rebellion.

6. James Madison, Alexander Hamilton, and John Jay wrote the *Federalist Papers* to support ratification of the Constitution.

K. THE BILL OF RIGHTS

1. The Federalists pledged that they would support adding a Bill of Rights to the Constitution to protect specific individual liberties from the control of a powerful central government.

2. The First Amendment guarantees freedom of religion, speech, and the press. It also guarantees the right of people to peaceably assemble and to petition the Government for "a redress of grievances."

3. It is important to note that the Bill of Rights does NOT include the right of all citizens to vote.

CHAPTER 8
THE FEDERALIST ERA, 1789–1800

A. HAMILTON'S FINANCIAL PLAN

1. President George Washington asked his Secretary of Treasury, Alexander Hamilton, to prepare a financial program that would promote the young nation's economic growth.
2. Hamilton's program included a number of bold proposals, designed to strengthen America's finances and give commercial interests a stake in the new government.
3. It is important to note that Hamilton's policies favored rich merchants and manufacturers.
4. Hamilton proposed that the federal government fund or "assume" the $65 million debt it owned to foreign and domestic creditors. He argued that a national debt would be beneficial, because it would tie the interests of the wealthy to America's continued success.
5. QUOTE: "A national debt if it is not excessive will be to us a national blessing, it will be a powerful cement of our union." Alexander Hamilton

B. THE NATIONAL BANK DEBATE

1. Hamilton recommended that Congress create a national bank to take care of the government's money and to lend funds to the government when necessary. It is interesting to note that in 1789, there were only three banks in the entire country.
2. Hamilton was a LOOSE CONSTRUCTIONIST who favored a broad interpretation of the Constitution. He used the implied powers of the necessary and proper clause to justify creating a national bank. Hamilton argued that what the Constitution does not forbid, it permits.

3. In contrast, Thomas Jefferson was a **STRICT CONSTRUCTIONIST** who favored a narrow interpretation of the Constitution. He admitted that a national bank would be convenient and useful. However, Jefferson insisted that a national bank was not absolutely necessary. He argued that what the Constitution does not permit, it forbids.

4. Hamilton's argument prevailed, and President Washington signed the bill into law, thus chartering the First National Bank of the United States.

C. HAMILTON VERSUS JEFFERSON

1. The national bank was just one of several issues that divided Hamilton and Jefferson. For example, Hamilton favored commercial and manufacturing interests, while Jefferson extolled the virtues of an agrarian or rural way of life.

2. It is important to note that both Hamilton and Jefferson believed that America should be governed by an aristocracy of talent.

D. THE WHISKEY REBELLION

1. Hamilton's financial program included an excise tax on whiskey, designed to raise revenue.

2. The tax ignited protests by backcountry farmers in Pennsylvania who resented the dominance of eastern commercial interests in the federal government.

3. Washington quickly suppressed the Whiskey Rebellion, thus demonstrating the power and authority of the new federal government.

4. It is interesting to note that opposition to tax policies sparked both the Whiskey Rebellion and Shays' Rebellion.

E. WASHINGTON'S FAREWELL ADDRESS

1. In his famous farewell address to the nation in 1796, President Washington urged future American leaders to avoid forming permanent alliances with foreign nations.

2. QUOTE: "The great rule of conduct for us in regard to foreign nations is, in extending our commercial relations, to have with them as little political connection as possible." George Washington

3. Opponents of the League of Nations used Washington's admonition to avoid entangling alliances to justify their opposition to the League.
4. During the 1930s, isolationists used Washington's Farewell Address to justify their support for neutrality laws.

F. THE ALIEN AND SEDITION ACTS

1. President John Adams inherited an undeclared Quasi-War with France. Adams resisted enormous political pressure to declare war on France.
2. The Federalist-controlled Congress took advantage of the anti-French furor to pass a series of laws known as the Alien and Sedition Acts. These acts were intended to silence Adams' critics.

G. THE KENTUCKY AND VIRGINIA RESOLUTIONS

1. Thomas Jefferson and James Madison believed that the Alien and Sedition Acts embodied a threat to individual liberties caused by unchecked Federalist power. They wrote a series of resolutions that were then approved by the state legislatures in Kentucky and Virginia.
2. The resolutions formulated a STATES' RIGHTS doctrine asserting that the Constitution arose as a compact among sovereign states. The states therefore retained the power to challenge and if necessary nullify federal laws.
3. John C. Calhoun and other Southerners later used this states' rights doctrine to support their own theory of nullification.
4. The Kentucky and Virginia Resolutions sparked a debate between strict and loose constructionists. Looking ahead, this debate recurred again over the Louisiana Purchase. However, it did NOT recur in the debate over the Gadsden Purchase.

CHAPTER 9
THE JEFFERSONIANS, 1801–1816

A. THE ELECTION OF 1800

1. The election of 1800 is often called "The Revolution of 1800," because it marked a peaceful transfer of political power from the Federalists, led by John Adams, to the Democratic-Republicans, led by Thomas Jefferson.
2. The election signaled the end of the Federalist Era.

B. JEFFERSONIAN DEMOCRACY

1. Jefferson wanted America to become an agrarian republic. He believed that independent farmers were the most productive and trustworthy citizens.
2. Jefferson promised to replace the formal ceremonies that characterized the Federalist administration with what he called "republican simplicity." For example, Jefferson used a round table in the White House dining room to avoid seating his guests by rank.
3. Jefferson believed that the government is best that governs least. Determined to practice "a wise and frugal government," he ended the excise tax on whiskey and cut the military budget.
4. Jefferson believed that freedom of speech is essential to a healthy republic. He urged Congress to repeal the Alien and Sedition Acts.
5. Jefferson did NOT believe that a strong army is essential to keep order.

C. THE LOUISIANA PURCHASE, 1803

1. In 1803, the French leader Napoleon Bonaparte offered to sell the entire Louisiana Territory to the United States for just $15 million.
2. Jefferson now faced a dilemma. He recognized that Napoleon's offer was too good to pass up. However, as a strict constructionist, Jefferson worried that the Constitution did not give Congress the power to purchase new territory. He therefore proposed a constitutional amendment giving Congress the needed power.
3. QUOTE: "This treaty must of course be laid before both Houses, because both have important functions to exercise respecting it. They, I presume, will see their duty to their country in ratifying and paying for it, so as to secure a goal which would otherwise probably be never again in their power. But I suppose they must then appeal to the nation for an additional article to the Constitution, approving and confirming an act which the nation had not previously authorized."
4. Despite his reservations, Jefferson recognized that he had to act quickly. Congress therefore promptly passed the treaty and Jefferson signed it.
5. The Louisiana Territory doubled the size of the United States. It is interesting to note that the Louisiana Territory is even bigger than Alaska!

D. THE LEWIS AND CLARK EXPEDITION

1. The Lewis and Clark expedition mapped the upper reaches of the Missouri River, explored the Columbia River, strengthened American claims to the Oregon Territory, and increased general scientific knowledge about northwestern America.
2. The Lewis and Clark expedition did NOT explore the Hudson River.

E. THE EMBARGO OF 1807

1. The Embargo Act of 1807 forbade American ships from trading with foreign nations. Jefferson hoped that the embargo would enable the United States to remain neutral in the European conflict raging between Great Britain and France.
2. The embargo proved to be very unpopular with New England shippers, who vehemently argued that it was unconstitutional.
3. The Embargo Act had the unforeseen effect of promoting American manufacturing.

F. THE MARSHALL COURT

1. Chief Justice John Marshall believed that he could best serve America by rendering judicial decisions that supported a strong central government and promoted business enterprise.
2. The Marshall Court established the principle of JUDICIAL REVIEW in *Marbury v. Madison*. Judicial review gave the Supreme Court the power to determine if a law conforms to the Constitution.

G. TECUMSEH AND TENSKWATAWA

1. Tecumseh and his brother Tenskwatawa were charismatic Indian leaders who formed a confederation of tribes in a determined effort to prevent the further loss of territory in the Old Northwest.
2. Tecumseh and Tenskwatawa successfully united a number of tribes on the eve of the War of 1812.

H. CAUSES OF THE WAR OF 1812

1. Led by Henry Clay, the War Hawks were expansionists who eagerly supported a war with Great Britain. They hoped to annex Canada, safeguard the frontier from British and Indian attacks, and defend American honor.
2. It is important to note that New England commercial interests did NOT support going to war with Great Britain.
3. The War Hawks did NOT want to protect Native Americans.

I. CONSEQUENCES OF THE WAR OF 1812

1. The War of 1812 promoted an increase in domestic manufacturing, intensified a spirit of national unity, and led to the demise of the Federalist Party.
2. The American victory at the Battle of New Orleans catapulted Andrew Jackson into a national hero.
3. Although the War Hawks had hoped to acquire new lands, the War of 1812 did NOT result in any new territorial gains for the United States.
4. The War of 1812 did NOT prompt the United States to build a two-ocean navy.

CHAPTER 10
THE ERA OF GOOD FEELINGS, 1816–1824

A. JAMES MONROE

1. James Monroe easily defeated his Federalist opponents in the 1816 presidential election.
2. One Boston newspaper captured the optimistic spirit of the time when it proclaimed that Monroe's election marked the beginning of a period of national unity that it called "The Era of Good Feelings."
3. It is important to note that Monroe's election coincided with the demise of the Federalist Party. As a result, there was an absence of competition between political parties during his administration.

B. THE ADAMS-ONIS TREATY, 1819

1. Negotiated with Spain, the Adams-Onis Treaty gave both East and West Florida to the United States.
2. The treaty also defined the western boundary of the Louisiana Purchase.

C. THE MISSOURI COMPROMISE, 1820

1. In 1819, the territory of Missouri applied for statehood as a slave state. At that time the Senate was evenly divided between 11 free states and 11 slave states.
2. House Speaker Henry Clay proposed a compromise that would preserve the balance in the Senate, by admitting Missouri as a slave state and Maine as a free state.
3. In addition, the Missouri Compromise closed the remaining territory of the Louisiana Purchase above 36°30′ north latitude to slavery. It is important to note that the North viewed this line as a "sacred pact" that should never be broken.

4. The Missouri Compromise temporarily defused the political crisis over slavery. However, the contentious debate over slavery did add a discordant note to the Era of Good Feelings.

D. THE MONROE DOCTRINE, 1823

1. In his final message to Congress on December 2, 1823, President Monroe announced a new American policy that later became known as the Monroe Doctrine. Fear of French intervention in the Western Hemisphere helped motivate Monroe's declaration.
2. Monroe's UNILATERAL declaration of principles declared that republican governments in the Americas were different and separate from the monarchical systems in Europe. As the protector of republican institutions, the United States would not tolerate the creation of new European colonies in the Western Hemisphere. Monroe further demanded that the European powers stay out of the internal affairs of the newly independent American nations.
3. In return, Monroe promised that the United States would not interfere with any established European colonies in the Western Hemisphere or in the internal affairs of any European nation.
4. The Monroe Doctrine did NOT express a desire for the United States to form a formal alliance with Great Britain.

E. THE AMERICAN SYSTEM

1. Sponsored by Senator Henry Clay of Kentucky, the American System supported the national bank to promote economic stability, called for a tariff to raise revenue and protect American industries, and the construction of a network of canals and roads to unite the country.
2. It is important to remember that the term INTERNAL IMPROVEMENTS referred to transportation projects.
3. Clay's American System was similar to Alexander Hamilton's economic vision. Both programs favored a strong federal government to promote commerce and economic growth.

F. THE TRANSPORTATION REVOLUTION

1. Canals and steamboats revolutionized American economic life during the Era of Good Feelings.
2. Steamboats sharply lowered the cost of transporting goods and led to a dramatic rise in traffic on Midwestern rivers.
3. The Erie Canal connected Buffalo with New York City. The canal enabled farmers near the Great Lakes to sell their produce to urban markets along the east coast.
4. The Erie Canal increased the size of both Buffalo and New York City. In addition, it dramatically lowered the cost of shipping goods between Buffalo and New York City. It therefore did NOT raise prices in these two cities.
5. The first railroad line opened in 1829, at the end of the Era of Good Feelings.

CHAPTER 11
THE AGE OF JACKSON, 1824–1840

A. THE ELECTION OF ANDREW JACKSON

1. Andrew Jackson and his fervent supporters felt cheated when the House of Representatives chose John Quincy Adams as President in 1824.
2. Jackson's supporters redoubled their campaign in the 1828 election. Old Hickory's reputation as a military hero played a major role in his overwhelming electoral victory.

B. JACKSONIAN DEMOCRACY

1. Jackson's election marked the beginning of a new era in American political history. As a self-made soldier, politician, and planter, Jackson was an example of what an able person without privileges might become in the United States.
2. Jackson's supporters hailed him as a champion of the common man, who would fight against special privileges in American life. It is interesting to note that Jackson's status as a wealthy planter was at odds with his image as a common man.
3. Jackson enthusiastically supported a SPOILS SYSTEM, by which he rewarded loyal supporters with government jobs.
4. Jackson's commitment to the common man also included his support for universal white male suffrage.
5. During the Jacksonian Era, party conventions replaced Congressional caucuses as vehicles for nominating candidates for president.

6. Like Presidents Madison and Monroe, Jackson thought that the federal government should not support internal improvements that were entirely local. He therefore vetoed the Maysville Road Bill, because it called for the federal government to help pay for a road that would be built entirely in Kentucky. Jackson's veto provides a good example of strict constructionism.

C. THE BANK WAR

1. The Second Bank of the United States included a main office and 25 branches. Jackson and his supporters assailed the bank as a "monster" that concentrated special financial advantages in the hands of a few privileged people.
2. The 20-year charter of the Second Bank of the United States was scheduled to expire in 1836. In July 1832, Jackson vetoed a bill that would have rechartered the bank. He denounced the bank as a vehicle used by "the rich and powerful to bend the acts of government to their selfish purposes."
3. Jackson's war against the bank played a key role in the creation of a new two-party system. Democrats opposed to the bank supported Jackson. In contrast, the Whigs supported the bank and opposed Jackson.

D. THE TARIFF OF ABOMINATIONS

1. High tariffs ignited passionate political debates during the 1830s. Led by South Carolina, Southern states vehemently opposed the so-called Tariff of Abominations because it raised the average duty to 50 percent of the value of imports.
2. South Carolina bitterly complained that the high tariffs forced them to pay exorbitant prices for imported goods.

E. JOHN C. CALHOUN AND THE DOCTRINE OF NULLIFICATION

1. Led by John C. Calhoun, Southern leaders advanced a theory of NULLIFICATION that gave any state the right to declare a federal law inoperative within its borders.
2. Calhoun based his theory on the states' rights arguments first formulated in the Virginia and Kentucky Resolutions.

3. President Jackson angrily denounced nullification as an "impractical absurdity" and called upon Congress to pass a "Force Bill" authorizing him to use the army to enforce federal laws in South Carolina.
4. As tensions mounted, Henry Clay proposed a new compromise tariff that would gradually reduce duties over the next ten years. The compromise worked, and South Carolina rescinded its nullification ordinance.

F. THE INDIAN REMOVAL ACT

1. In the late 1820s approximately 125,000 Native Americans lived east of the Mississippi River. They were often surrounded by white settlers who wanted their land.
2. Supported by President Jackson, Congress passed the Indian Removal Act, providing for the exchange of Indian lands in the East for government lands in the newly established Indian Territory.

G. *WORCESTER V. GEORGIA*, 1832

1. The Cherokee legally challenged the removal order. In *Worcester v. Georgia*, Chief Justice John Marshall upheld the Cherokee Nation's legal right to their ancestral land.
2. President Jackson refused to enforce the Supreme Court decision, declaring, "John Marshall has made his decision, now let him enforce it."
3. QUOTE: "I have long viewed treaties with American Indians as an absurdity not to be reconciled to the principles of our government." Andrew Jackson

H. THE TRAIL OF TEARS, 1838

1. In 1838, about 7,000 federal troops began the forcible evacuation of some 17,000 Cherokee from their lands in northwestern Georgia to Oklahoma.
2. As many as one-fourth of the Cherokee died on the 116-day forced march along what became known as the Trail of Tears.

CHAPTER 12
REFORM AND REFORMERS, 1800–1850

A. THE SECOND GREAT AWAKENING

1. The SECOND GREAT AWAKENING was a wave of religious enthusiasm that spread across American in the early 19th century.
2. Charles Grandison Finney was the best known and most influential Second Great Awakening preacher.
3. The Burned-Over District was an area in western New York where Finney and other preachers delivered "hellfire and damnation" sermons that aroused intense religious zeal.
4. The Second Great Awakening stressed that each individual was a moral free agent, who could improve both himself and society.
5. The Second Great Awakening inspired a belief in PERFECTIONISM—the faith in the human ability to build a just society.
6. The Second Great Awakening inspired a generation of social reformers who worked to abolish slavery, promote women's rights, limit the sale of alcoholic beverages, restrict commerce on Sunday, reform insane asylums, and improve public schools. Reformers did NOT work for black suffrage.

B. TRANSCENDENTALISM

1. TRANSCENDENTALISM was a philosophical and literary movement that stressed the importance of intuition, nonconformity, and the belief that truth could be found in nature.
2. Ralph Waldo Emerson, Henry David Thoreau, and Margaret Fuller were the leading transcendentalists. It is important to remember that Edgar Allan Poe was NOT a transcendentalist.

3. QUOTE: "The height, the deity of man is to be self-sustained, to need no gift, no foreign force. Society, is good when it does not violate me, but best when it is likest to solitude." Ralph Waldo Emerson

C. THE HUDSON RIVER SCHOOL

1. A group of artists known as the Hudson River School applied the transcendentalist reverence for nature to art.
2. Hudson River School artists painted landscape paintings that idealized the beauty of the American countryside.

D. ROMANTIC LITERATURE

1. Like the Hudson School artists, Romantic poets looked to nature for insights about truth and beauty.
2. Walt Whitman was America's leading Romantic poet. His famous volume of poems, *Leaves of Grass*, rejected reason and favored feeling and emotion.
3. In his poem "When I Heard the Learn'd Astronomer," Whitman argued that a Romantic perspective can yield deeper insights about truth and beauty than a scientific perspective.

E. UTOPIAN COMMUNITIES

1. Idealists founded over 100 utopian communities, where they tried new ways of organizing work and daily life.
2. Utopian communities rejected competitive business practices, favored communal living arrangements, opposed strict moral rules, and shared wealth.
3. Brook Farm and Oneida were two of the best known utopian communities.
4. Utopian communities did NOT adopt Native American traditions or agitate for political secession.

F. KEY REFORMERS

1. Dorothea Dix led a crusade to create special hospitals for the mentally ill. It is important to note that she did NOT participate in the struggle for women's rights.
2. Horace Mann was a leader in the movement to reform and improve the nation's public schools.

G. NATIVISM

1. Many reformers were attracted to NATIVISM, an anti-immigrant movement that began to grow in strength in the 1840s.
2. The 1840s witnessed a massive migration of Irish and German immigrants to the United States.
3. The Irish typically settled in port cities in the Northeast, while the Germans settled in the Midwest. It is important to note that few immigrants settled in the South, because they could not compete with slave labor.
4. Many Protestants joined the Know-Nothing Party to express their hostility toward Catholic immigrants from Ireland and Germany.
5. The Know-Nothings became America's first nativist political party. They directed particular hostility toward the Irish, often posting signs in shops that read, "NO IRISH NEED APPLY."
6. QUOTE: "Americans must rule America; and it is to this end, native-born citizens should be selected for all state, federal, or municipal offices of government employment, in preference to naturalized citizens." Platform of the Know-Nothing Party
7. QUOTE: "The Irish are making our elections scenes of violence and fraud...Americans! Shall we be ruled by Irish and Germans?" A Know-Nothing political handbill

CHAPTER 13
THE STRUGGLE FOR WOMEN'S RIGHTS, 1800–1850

A. A LACK OF RIGHTS

1. Although the new American republic promoted equality and social democracy, laws forbade women from voting, holding political office, or serving on juries.
2. A married woman had no separate legal identity apart from her husband.

B. REPUBLICAN MOTHERHOOD

1. Although American women lacked basic civic rights, they did have a vital role to play in shaping America's moral and political character.
2. According to the idea of REPUBLICAN MOTHERHOOD, American women had a duty to use their moral influence to raise their children to be virtuous and responsible citizens.
3. QUOTE: "The mother writes the character of the future man; the sister bends the fibres that hereafter are the forest tree; the wife sways the heart, whose energies may turn for good or for evil the destinies of a nation. Let the women of a country be virtuous and intelligent, and the men will certainly be the same." Catharine Beecher

C. THE CULT OF DOMESTICITY

1. The CULT OF DOMESTICITY idealized women in their roles as wives and mothers.
2. The cult of domesticity applied to upper- and middle-class white families that could afford to maintain separate spheres for their work and home lives.
3. The cult of domesticity did NOT work well for women employed in factories or for enslaved black women.

4. It is important to note that the SAT II often uses a picture to test your ability to identify the cult of domesticity. The picture typically shows a cultured upper-middle-class mother surrounded by her children, who are playing musical instruments and reading literature. Needless to say, her husband stands to the side, nodding his approval.

D. THE LOWELL TEXTILE FACTORY

1. America's textile industry took root in small towns outside of Boston. The early textile industry benefitted from the presence of fast-moving streams that provided water power, the reduction of British textiles caused by the Embargo Act of 1807, and by a surplus of single women in the region's rural population. Railroads did NOT play a role in the early growth of the textile industry.

2. Textile mills in Lowell employed a large number of young women who wanted to be independent and earn their own income.

3. The Lowell factory provided special chaperoned dormitories for its women workers.

4. The Lowell experiment with working women experienced a major setback when the women went out on strike to protest a cut in their wages without a reduction in their working hours. Factory owners soon replaced the women with impoverished Irish immigrants, then pouring into Massachusetts.

E. THE SENECA FALLS CONVENTION, 1848

1. In 1848, Elizabeth Cady Stanton and Lucretia Mott organized the first convention to demand increased rights for women. The convention met for two days in Seneca Falls, New York.

2. The convention issued a "Declaration of Sentiments" that opened by declaring, "We hold these truths to be self-evident: that all men and women are created equal."

3. The Declaration of Sentiments called for greater divorce and child custody rights, equal opportunities in education, the right to retain property after marriage, and the extension of suffrage to women.

4. The Declaration of Sentiments did NOT call for equal pay for equal work or for greater access to birth control methods.

F. THE TEMPERANCE MOVEMENT

1. Women played a key role in the temperance movement to convince Americans to drink fewer alcoholic beverages.
2. Their campaign against "Demon Rum" worked. By the mid-1840s, annual consumption of alcohol dropped from five to two gallons per person.

CHAPTER 14
THE COTTON KINGDOM, SLAVERY, AND THE FIRST ABOLITIONISTS, 1793–1860

A. THE RISE OF THE COTTON KINGDOM

1. Tobacco dominated the Southern economy during the colonial period. However, tobacco sales did NOT increase after the Revolutionary War.

2. The Industrial Revolution and the rise of textile manufacturing in England created an insatiable demand for raw cotton.

3. In 1793, Eli Whitney invented a machine that could separate cotton fiber from its sticky seeds. His cotton gin enabled slaves to separate 50 times as much cotton as could be done by hand. (It is interesting to note that Whitney later invented the technique of using interchangeable parts to manufacture guns.)

4. Cotton quickly became America's most valuable cash crop. By 1840, cotton production accounted for more than half of the value of all American exports.

5. As cotton profits soared, planters expanded cotton production to rich new lands in the Deep South. Soon a vast cotton belt stretched from eastern North Carolina to the Mississippi River Valley. Proud Southern planters boasted that "Cotton is King."

6. It is important to note that canals and railroads had little impact on the South's cotton economy. Additionally, the spread of slavery was NOT related to slaves having any prior experience picking cotton in Africa.

B. COTTON AND SLAVERY

1. The rapid expansion of cotton production firmly tied the South to the institution of slavery.
2. Congress ended the slave trade in 1808. As a result, planters could no longer import slaves from Africa or the West Indies. Instead they bought slaves from planters in Virginia and Maryland. Between 1810 and 1860, over two million slaves endured a forced migration from the Chesapeake area to the slaveholding states in the Deep South.
3. Southern planters now insisted that their "peculiar institution" was in fact a "positive good." They argued that benevolent planters cared for their slaves' wellbeing and converted them to Christianity. However, the positive good proponents did NOT argue that the slaves had more access to education.

C. WHITE SOCIETY IN THE OLD SOUTH

1. The majority of white families in the antebellum or pre-Civil War South did NOT own any slaves.
2. Most white Southerners were small farmers. Just one in four Southern families owned slaves.
3. Planters comprised just four percent of the Southern adult male population. This small but powerful group owned more than half of all the slaves. They dominated the region's economy and cultural life.

D. KEY FACTS ABOUT SLAVE LIFE IN THE OLD SOUTH

1. In the half-century before the Civil War, the number of slaves increased from 1.2 million to just under four million. Much of this increase was due to the natural population increase of American-born slaves.
2. Historical evidence indicates that most slaves responded to their conditions by creating a separate African American culture.
3. Most Southern slaves did NOT resist their masters by outright armed rebellion. Instead, they often slowed the pace of their work and feigned illness. Slaves did NOT rebel by intermarrying.

4. Blacks living in the South were NOT all slaves. By 1860, as many as 250,000 free blacks lived in the South. These freedmen were able to accumulate some property despite continued discrimination.

E. THE AMERICAN COLONIZATION SOCIETY

1. The American Colonization Society (ACS) launched the first organized anti-slavery movement in the United States. The ACS proposed to ship freed slaves back to Africa.
2. The Society's gradual approach could not solve the rapidly growing problem of slavery. By 1860, the Society helped just 12,000 blacks return to Africa, out of a total slave population of four million.

F. WILLIAM LLOYD GARRISON

1. William Lloyd Garrison was originally inspired by the Second Great Awakening's emphasis upon social improvement. He repudiated the ACS's moderate approach as both too slow and too impractical.
2. Garrison published *The Liberator*, an antislavery newspaper dedicated to the immediate and uncompensated abolition of slavery. He attacked slavery as both a violation of American democratic principles and a sin that had to be eliminated.
3. QUOTE: "Let Southern oppressors tremble...I shall strenuously contend for immediate enfranchisement...I will be as harsh as truth, and as uncompromising as justice...I do not wish to think, or speak, or write with moderation—I will not excuse—I will not retreat a single inch—AND I WILL BE HEARD!"
4. Garrison's uncompromising call for immediate and uncompensated emancipation marked the beginning of the radical movement to abolish slavery and transform American society.
5. It is important to note that the abolitionist movement included a number of women who also worked for women's rights.

6. The growing anti-slavery agitation prompted angry Southerners in the House of Representatives to enact a Gag Resolution requiring all antislavery resolutions to be tabled without debate. Led by John Quincy Adams, outraged Northern representatives finally repealed the "gag rule."

G. FREDERICK DOUGLASS

1. Frederick Douglass was the best-known and most effective black abolitionist.
2. Douglass told the story of his life as a slave in an autobiography that helped illustrate slavery's inhumanity.

CHAPTER 15
THE GATHERING STORM, 1836–1850

A. THE TEXAS ANNEXATION ISSUE, 1836

1. The Texas Republic successfully declared its independence in 1836. Led by Sam Houston, Texas wanted to become part of the United States.
2. The Texas constitution allowed slavery. Northern antislavery Whigs strongly opposed admitting another slave state into the Union.
3. President Jackson feared that a prolonged debate over the annexation of a slave state would ignite a divisive campaign issue that could cost the Democratic candidate, Martin Van Buren, the presidency. Jackson therefore postponed annexation, and Texas remained an independent "Lone Star Republic."

B. MANIFEST DESTINY

1. John L. O'Sullivan coined the term MANIFEST DESTINY to express his belief that America was foreordained to extend its civilization across the North American continent.
2. QUOTE: "By the right of our manifest destiny to overspread and to possess the whole of the continent which Providence has given us for the development of the great experiment of liberty and federated self-government entrusted to us." John L. O'Sullivan
3. During the 1840s, advocates of westward expansion used the Manifest Destiny slogan to support U.S. territorial acquisitions to Oregon and the Pacific Coast.
4. It is important to note that New England abolitionists opposed Manifest Destiny, because they feared it would lead to the spread of slavery to newly acquired territory.

C. JAMES K. POLK

1. The annexation of Texas and territorial expansion emerged as the key issues in the 1844 presidential campaign.
2. The Democratic Party nominee, James K. Polk, ran on a platform demanding the annexation of Texas, claiming all of Oregon, and offering to purchase California.
3. Polk and his Democratic supporters used the slogan "Fifty-four forty or fight" to emphasize their willingness to fight Great Britain to obtain all of the Oregon Territory up to its northernmost boundary.

D. TEXAS AND OREGON

1. Following the election of Polk, Congress approved a resolution annexing Texas as the nation's 28th state. Texas thus entered the Union as a slave state.
2. Despite his belligerent campaign slogan, Polk agreed to a compromise with Great Britain that divided Oregon at the 49th parallel.

E. THE MEXICAN WAR

1. Although Polk carefully avoided a war with Great Britain, he eagerly entered a war with Mexico. Polk claimed that deliberate Mexican incursions into land claimed by the United States justified a declaration of war.
2. Whigs and New England abolitionists denounced the Mexican War as an unjust conflict, designed to extend slavery into the new territories.

F. THE TREATY OF GUADALUPE HIDALGO

1. Mexico ceded New Mexico and California to the United States and accepted the Rio Grande River as the Texas border.
2. The later Gadsden Purchase was NOT part of the Treaty of Guadalupe Hidalgo and did NOT play a role in exacerbating sectional tensions. The purchase included land in the southern portion of the New Mexico Territory that would facilitate the construction of a transcontinental railroad connecting Houston, Texas, with Los Angeles, California.

G. THE WILMOT PROVISO

1. The Wilmot Proviso called for the prohibition of slavery in the lands acquired from Mexico in the Mexican War.
2. The House of Representatives did vote to pass the Wilmot Proviso. However, the South successfully blocked the proviso in the Senate. The Wilmot Proviso thus did NOT become a law.

H. THE COMPROMISE OF 1850

1. Stephen Douglas, Daniel Webster, Henry Clay, and John C. Calhoun were all involved in negotiations that resulted in the passage of the Compromise of 1850.
2. Abraham Lincoln was NOT involved in these negotiations, because he was not a member of Congress at that time.
3. The Compromise of 1850 included the following provisions:
   - The admission of California as a free state.
   - The establishment of territorial governments in New Mexico and Utah without an immediate decision as to whether they would be free or slave.
   - The abolition of the slave trade in the District of Columbia.
   - The enactment of a stringent Fugitive Slave Act. This act proved to be the most controversial part of the Compromise of 1850.
4. The Compromise of 1850 did NOT recognize Kansas and Nebraska as states of the Union regardless of their policies on slavery.
5. Supporters hoped that the Compromise of 1850 would defuse the contentious issue of slavery in the territories. However, these hopes proved to be in vain.

CHAPTER 16
THE NATION DIVIDES, 1850–1860

A. *UNCLE TOM'S CABIN*

1. The rising furor over the Fugitive Slave Act inspired Harriet Beecher Stowe to write *Uncle Tom's Cabin*.
2. *Uncle Tom's Cabin* proved to be a bestseller that sold more copies than any other book except the Bible.
3. *Uncle Tom's Cabin* intensified Northern opposition to slavery.

B. STEPHEN A. DOUGLAS AND POPULAR SOVEREIGNTY

1. Senator Stephen A. Douglas of Illinois reopened the issue of slavery in the territories.
2. It is important to remember that both the Kansas and Nebraska territories were located in the part of the Louisiana Territory where the Missouri Compromise banned slavery.
3. Douglas proposed to allow the people of Kansas and Nebraska to decide for themselves if their states would become free or slave. Letting settlers in a given territory have the sole right to decide whether or not slavery would be permitted within their borders was known as POPULAR SOVEREIGNTY.
4. QUOTE: "The great principle is the right of every community to judge and decide for itself whether a thing is right or wrong...It is no answer to this argument to say that slavery is an evil, and hence should not be tolerated. You must allow the people to decide for themselves whether it is a good or an evil." Stephen A. Douglas

C. THE KANSAS-NEBRASKA ACT, 1854

1. Douglas proposed a bill called the Kansas-Nebraska Act to organize the Kansas and Nebraska territories based upon the principle of popular sovereignty.
2. Congress passed the Kansas-Nebraska Act after a long and bitter debate. Douglas underestimated the roar of public outrage in the North.
3. The Kansas-Nebraska Act had several momentous consequences:
   - It effectively repealed the Missouri Compromise ban on the extension of slavery into the Louisiana Territory.
   - It galvanized a spontaneous outpouring of popular opposition in the North that led to the formation of the Republican Party.
   - It led to the demise of the Whig Party.
   - It split the Democratic Party into Northern and Southern wings.
4. Kansas soon became the first test of popular sovereignty.

D. THE DRED SCOTT DECISION, 1857

1. Dred Scott was a slave who had been bought in Missouri. His owner later took Scott to the free state of Illinois. Eventually, Scott's owner returned to Missouri. After his owner died, Scott claimed to be a free man because he had once lived in a free state.
2. Led by Chief Justice Roger Taney, the Supreme Court ruled that Dred Scott and all other African American slaves and freedmen were NOT citizens and therefore could not petition the Court.
3. The Taney Court also ruled that Congress had no right to prohibit slavery in the territories, thus striking down both the Northwest Ordinance and the Missouri Compromise.
4. The Dred Scott decision allowed the possibility of extending slavery into any of the western territories.
5. The Dred Scott decision became a major issue in the Lincoln-Douglas debates.

E. JOHN BROWN'S RAID ON HARPER'S FERRY, 1859

1. John Brown's raid on Harper's Ferry intensified sectional bitterness. The raid touched a highly sensitive nerve by convincing outraged Southerners that the North wanted to provoke a slave revolt.
2. Although his raid was a military failure, John Brown became a martyr for the antislavery cause.

F. THE ELECTION OF 1860

1. The 1860 Republican Party platform accepted slavery in the states where it existed. However, the Republicans opposed any further extension of slavery into any of the western territories. The Democrats were divided on this issue.
2. The Republican presidential candidate Abraham Lincoln won the 1860 presidential election by carrying only states in the North plus California and Oregon. Lincoln failed to win any of the border states or states in the South.
3. Lincoln's election prompted South Carolina and six other Deep South states to secede from the Union.

G. THE CRITTENDEN COMPROMISE

1. In a final desperate effort to save the Union, Senator John Crittenden of Kentucky proposed to restore the boundary line between free and slave states established by the Missouri Compromise of 1820.
2. Lincoln rejected the Crittenden Compromise because it violated the Republican Party's firm position against the further extension of slavery into the Western territories.

CHAPTER 17
THE CIVIL WAR, 1861–1865

A. THE NORTH–KEY FACTS

1. The North's industrial dominance and economic strength proved to be a decisive advantage in its victory over the South.
2. Northern advantages did NOT include having a supply of raw cotton to manufacture textiles.
3. President Lincoln invoked the Suspension Clause of the United States Constitution to suspend the right of habeas corpus in Maryland.
4. During the Civil War the Republican-dominated Congress enacted high tariffs, organized a national banking system with a uniform currency, and approved a transcontinental railroad.
5. The Republican Congress passed the Morrill Land Grant Act, stipulating that public lands be donated to states for providing colleges to train students in agriculture.
6. The Republican Congress passed the Homestead Act, opening the Great Plains to settlers.
7. The Republican-dominated Congress did NOT pass legislation abolishing slavery, making high school education mandatory, or granting government subsidies to encourage the export of manufactured goods.

B. THE SOUTH–KEY FACTS

1. The South had an experienced and talented group of military officers who fought most of the war's battles defending their homeland.
2. The South did NOT have an extensive rail network or strong industrial base.

3. Southern leaders did NOT effectively manage their region's economic resources. This failure was one of the key reasons the South lost the Civil War.
4. The North feared that Great Britain would actively support the Confederacy. However, the South failed to obtain diplomatic recognition and support from either Great Britain or France.

C. THE BORDER STATES–KEY FACTS

1. Maryland and Kentucky were border states that did NOT secede from the Union.
2. Lincoln's treatment of the border states proved that the original purpose of the Civil War was to preserve the Union and NOT to abolish slavery.
3. Kentucky's strategic location and important industrial and agricultural resources proved to be a key asset for the Union.

D. KEY BATTLES

1. The Union victory at Vicksburg gave the North control over the Mississippi River.
2. Confederate general Robert E. Lee successfully crossed the Mason-Dixon Line and reached into Pennsylvania. However, the Union victory at Gettysburg prevented Lee from cutting off key rail links and lowering Northern morale.
3. The Union victory at Atlanta and General William T. Sherman's subsequent March to the Sea dealt devastating blows to the South's economy and will to continue the war.
4. QUOTE: "We are not only fighting hostile armies, but a hostile people...We cannot change the hearts of those people... but we can make war so terrible... and make them so sick of war that generations would pass away before they would appeal again to it...If we can march a well-appointed army right through the enemy's territory, it is a demonstration to the world, foreign and domestic that we have a power which the enemy cannot resist. This may not be war, but rather statesmanship." General William T. Sherman

E. THE EMANCIPATION PROCLAMATION, 1863

1. The Union victory at Antietam persuaded England and France to remain neutral.
2. The Union victory at Antietam enabled Lincoln to issue the Emancipation Proclamation.
3. The Emancipation Proclamation only freed slaves in Confederate states that were still in rebellion. It did NOT free slaves in the border states.

F. THE NEW YORK CITY DRAFT RIOTS, 1863

1. Poor Irish immigrants in New York City opposed President Lincoln, the military draft, and the emancipation of slaves.
2. The draft riots convulsed New York City for days before it was finally suppressed by federal troops.
3. The draft riots underscored racial, economic, and cultural tensions in the North. Rioting Irish bitterly complained that the Civil War was "a rich man's war but a poor man's fight."

CHAPTER 18
RECONSTRUCTION AND THE OLD SOUTH, 1865–1900

A. THE RECONSTRUCTION AMENDMENTS
1. The Thirteenth Amendment, 1865
   - The Thirteenth Amendment abolished slavery in the United States.
   - The Thirteenth Amendment thus superseded the Emancipation Proclamation.
2. The Fourteenth Amendment, 1868
   - The Fourteenth Amendment granted citizenship to "all persons born or naturalized in the United States."
   - The Fourteenth Amendment thus negated the Dred Scott decision and the Three-Fifths Compromise.
   - The Fourteenth Amendment also forbade any State of depriving any "person of life, liberty, or property, without due process of law." It is important to remember that in the 1950s the Supreme Court used the "due process of law" clause to overturn Jim Crow segregation laws.
3. The Fifteenth Amendment, 1870
   - The Fifteenth Amendment gave African Americans the right to to vote.
   - QUOTE: "The right of citizens of the United States to vote shall not be denied or abridged by the United States or by any state on account of race, color, or previous condition of servitude." The Fifteenth Amendment
   - The Fifteenth Amendment outraged many women's rights activists who demanded to know why Congress granted suffrage to ex-slaves and NOT to women.

B. RADICAL RECONSTRUCTION

1. Between 1865 and 1877, the Radical Republicans supported the abolition of slavery, federal protection for civil rights, and voting rights for African American men. They did NOT support a reduction in tariff rates.
2. The Radical Republicans created the Freedmen's Bureau to help the newly freed slaves. The Freedmen's Bureau did NOT encourage African Americans to migrate to the North.
3. The Radical Republicans impeached President Andrew Johnson because he opposed and obstructed their Reconstruction plans. The Republican-dominated House of Representatives impeached Johnson for "high crimes and misdemeanors in office" that included violating the Tenure of Office Act. However, the Senate failed to convict Johnson by one vote.

C. CARPETBAGGERS AND SCALAWAGS

1. CARPETBAGGERS were Northerners who supposedly packed their belongings into a carpet suitcase and headed south to seek power and profit.
2. SCALAWAGS were Southerners who "betrayed" the South by voting for Republicans and then benefitting from Radical Republican policies.

D. THE PLIGHT OF AFRICAN AMERICANS

1. Slavery left a legacy of prejudice and discrimination that would be difficult to eliminate.
2. Unwilling to accept African Americans as equals, Southern legislatures enacted laws known as Black Codes to limit the freedmen's basic civil and economic rights. For example, Black Codes barred African Americans from carrying guns, marrying whites, assembling in groups, serving on juries, or pursuing any occupation other than agricultural work. It is important to note that the Black Codes created conditions reminiscent of slavery.
3. The Southern economy was still dependent upon cotton. Most African Americans became SHARECROPPERS who exchanged their labor for land, tools, and seed. The sharecroppers typically gave the landowner half of the crop as payment for using his property.

4. Sharecropping produced an endless cycle of debt and poverty.
5. EXODUSTERS was a name given to African Americans who left the South in 1879 and 1880 to begin a new life in Kansas.

E. THE COMPROMISE OF 1877

1. The presidential election of 1876, between the Republican candidate Rutherford B. Hayes and the Democratic candidate Samuel Tilden, created a potential constitutional crisis when Tilden won the popular vote but the electoral vote was disputed and thus unclear.
2. An electoral commission resolved the crisis by awarding the election to Hayes.
3. The Democrats accepted their decision in exchange for Republican promises to withdraw all federal soldiers from the South, appoint a Southerner to Hayes' Cabinet, and grant federal funds for internal improvements in the South. The Compromise of 1877 did NOT give money to Southern states to educate African Americans.
4. The Compromise of 1877 ended Reconstruction.

F. THE RISE OF JIM CROW SEGREGATION

1. The Compromise of 1877 left the South once again under the control of the same elites that had ruled the region during the antebellum period.
2. Southern legislatures soon passed a series of so-called Jim Crow laws that discriminated against African Americans by creating segregated facilities in virtually all aspects of daily life.
3. In the case of *Plessy v. Ferguson*, the Supreme Court ruled that segregated railroad cars in Louisiana were legal as long as the facilities were equal for both blacks and whites. This ruling created a doctrine known as "separate but equal."
4. The separate but equal ruling in *Plessy v. Ferguson* led to the creation of separate educational institutions for African Americans that remained in force until they were overturned by the Supreme Court in its landmark ruling in *Brown v. Board of Education*.

G. BOOKER T. WASHINGTON

1. Booker T. Washington was a well-known black leader who encouraged African Americans to focus on economic opportunities rather than political rights and social integration.
2. In a famous speech delivered at the opening of an international exhibition in Atlanta, Georgia, Washington promised his white audience that African Americans would be loyal and hard-working employees.
3. QUOTE: "In all things purely social we can be as separate as the fingers, yet one as the hand in all things essential to mutual progress." Booker T. Washington
4. In exchange for African American acceptance of the social and political order, Washington asked for white support for vocational programs that would provide black self-help and economic progress. African American self-help and vocational training thus became the hallmarks of Washington's program of racial accommodation.

H. W.E.B. Du BOIS

1. Not all African Americans agreed with Washington's accommodationist policies.
2. W.E.B. Du Bois sharply criticized Washington's speech, calling it the "Atlanta Compromise."
3. Du Bois supported the full economic, political, and social integration of African Americans into American society.
4. Du Bois advocated the development of a "talented tenth" of African Americans who would become a vanguard of influential leaders dedicated to an unceasing struggle for social change and civil rights.
5. Du Bois was one of the founders of the National Association for the Advancement of Colored People (NAACP). The organization focused on using the courts to strike down Jim Crow segregation laws.

I. THE NEW SOUTH

1. New South leaders called Redeemers supported the development of a diversified Southern economy that included an industrial base.
2. It is important to remember that the Redeemers also staunchly supported Jim Crow segregation laws and white supremacy.
3. The late 19th century witnessed a dramatic increase in the number of textile mills in the South.

CHAPTER 19
THE WEST, 1865-1900

A. THE MINERS' FRONTIER

1. A series of spectacular mining discoveries followed the California gold rush. For example, the Comstock Lode in Nevada yielded more than $300 million by 1879.

2. The early mining camps contained a heterogeneous mix of people that included American Indian, Mexican, Chinese, African American, and white miners.

3. Although a few individual miners struck it rich, most left with little or nothing.

4. QUOTE: "It has been several autumns now since your dull husband left you for a far remote alien land. Thanks to my hearty body I am alright...Because of our destitution I went out, trying to make a living. Who could know that Fate is always opposite to man's design? Because I can get no gold, I am detained in this secluded corner of a strange land." A Chinese migrant to the American mining frontier

5. When individual prospectors left the surface finds, large companies with money to buy equipment and hire workers took over the mining operations.

B. THE TRANSCONTINENTAL RAILROADS

1. Workers completed the first transcontinental railroad on May 10, 1869, when officials hammered in a last golden spike with a silver hammer. Many Chinese and Irish immigrants worked on this epic construction project.

2. Within a short time, other transcontinental railroads crisscrossed the West. These railroads made the Great Plains accessible to a dramatic surge in the region's population.

3. The transcontinental railroads also made it possible for hunters to nearly exterminate the vast herds of buffalo that once roamed the Great Plains. The destruction of the buffalo herds irrevocably altered the way of life of the Plains Indians.

C. THE COWBOYS' FRONTIER

1. By 1860, about five million head of longhorn cattle roamed the southwestern region of Texas. Meanwhile, fast-growing populations in Midwestern and Eastern cities demanded more and more meat.
2. Ambitious Texans drove huge herds of 2,000 to 2,500 steers along trails that stretched from Texas to railroad towns in Kansas. For example, the Chisholm Trail ran from ranches near San Antonio, Texas, to railroad lines in Abilene, Kansas.
3. The cattle drives ended in the late 1880s because of a combination of falling beef prices and bitterly cold winters that decimated the cattle herds. The cattle drives did NOT end because of falling demand for beef in the East.

D. THE FARMERS' FRONTIER

1. Between 1870 and 1900, more land in America was turned into farms than in the nation's previous 250-year history.
2. Barbed-wire fencing, wind-driven water pumps, iron plows, and reapers all contributed to the development of agriculture on the Great Plains.
3. Chemical fertilizers were NOT used during the late 19th century.

E. *A CENTURY OF DISHONOR*, 1881

1. Helen Hunt Jackson was an outspoken writer who championed the cause of Native Americans.
2. *A Century of Dishonor* documented the government's systematic mistreatment of Native Americans. Jackson castigated the United States government for its role in "a tale of wrongs and oppressions...that is too monstrous to be believed."

F. THE DAWES SEVERALTY ACT, 1887

1. *A Century of Dishonor* played a key role in mobilizing public support for a new Native American policy.
2. Congress passed the Dawes Severalty Act in 1887. The act attempted to "civilize" the Plains Indians by turning them into self-supporting farmers.
3. The Dawes Severalty Act divided tribal lands into individual homesteads of 160 acres that were then distributed to the head of each Indian family.
4. Intended to be a reform, the Dawes Severalty Act actually harmed the Plains Indians by dividing tribal lands into individual private farms. The Dawes Severalty Act cost the Plains Indians about two-thirds of their land.

G. THE GHOST DANCE

1. The slaughter of the buffalo caused an irrevocable disruption of Plains Indian culture.
2. Many desperate Native Americans performed a ritual Ghost Dance they believed would hasten the return of the buffalo and the departure of the white settlers.
3. Suspicious government agents wanted to suppress the Ghost Dance, because they feared that the Indians actually intended to go on the warpath.

H. TURNER'S FRONTIER THESIS

1. Frederick Jackson Turner was a young history professor at the University of Wisconsin.
2. In an essay entitled "The Significance of the Frontier in American History," Turner wrote that the frontier experience played a key role in promoting democratic institutions and in encouraging individualism.
3. QUOTE: "From the beginning of the settlement of America, the frontier regions have exercised influence toward democracy... American democracy is fundamentally the outcome of the experience of the American people in dealing with the West." Frederick Jackson Turner

CHAPTER 20
INDUSTRY AND LABOR, 1865–1900

A. VERTICAL AND HORIZONTAL INTEGRATION

1. VERTICAL INTEGRATION is the process by which a single company owns and controls the entire production process, from the unearthing of raw materials to the sale of finished products. Andrew Carnegie used vertical integration to gain control over the steel industry.

2. HORIZONTAL INTEGRATION is the process by which a company gains control of other firms that produce the same product. John D. Rockefeller used horizontal integration to gain control over oil prices and build the Standard Oil Company into a huge monopoly.

3. Led by Andrew Carnegie and John D. Rockefeller, American industrialists used vertical and horizontal integration to create powerful monopolies and trusts.

B. FREDERICK W. TAYLOR

1. Frederick Taylor was a prominent engineer who is called the "Father of Scientific Management."

2. TAYLORISM is the use of time-and-motion studies to eliminate wasted movements, reduce costs, and promote greater efficiency in factories and assembly lines.

3. QUOTE: "I hear the whistle. I must hurry. It is time to go into the shop. I change my clothes and get ready to work. The starting whistle blows." Excerpt from an industrial brochure used to promote Taylorism

C. SOCIAL DARWINISM

1. The industrial revolution and America's booming economy produced unprecedented personal fortunes. By 1900, the richest two percent of America's households owned over one-third of the nation's physical wealth.

2. SOCIAL DARWINISM was a set of beliefs that both explained and justified how a small group of business and industrial leaders could accumulate such great wealth.

3. Social Darwinists believed that Darwin's law of natural selection could be applied to individuals, corporations, and nations. According to the Social Darwinists, individuals and corporations are engaged in a ruthless struggle for profit in which only the fit prosper and survive.

4. QUOTE: "The growth of a large business corporation is merely survival of the fittest...The American Beauty rose can be produced in the splendor and fragrance which brings cheer to its beholder only by sacrificing the early buds which grow up around it. This is not an evil tendency in business. It is merely the working out of a law of nature and a law of God." John D. Rockefeller

5. QUOTE: "The human race began in utter destitution. It had no physical or metaphysical endowment whatever. The existing 'system' is the outcome of the efforts of men for thousands of years to work together, so as to win in the struggle for existence." William Graham Summer

6. Social Darwinists argued that the social and economic problems created by American industrial growth were part of a natural evolutionary process beyond human control.

7. Many late 19th-century advocates of Social Darwinism also favored a *laissez-faire* or "hands off" view that economic activity should be largely free of government regulation.

8. It is interesting to note that many of the same business leaders who favored Social Darwinism and the *laissez-faire* doctrine also welcomed government assistance in the form of high protective tariffs.

D. THE GOSPEL OF WEALTH

1. Andrew Carnegie was an ardent supporter of Social Darwinism who also believed that great wealth brought great responsibility.
2. In his 1889 essay, "The Gospel of Wealth," Carnegie encouraged philanthropists to support public libraries, universities, museums, and other "ladders upon which the aspiring can rise."
3. QUOTE: "This, then, is the duty of the man of wealth; to consider all surplus revenues which come to him simply as trust funds, which he is called upon to administer and strictly bound as a matter of duty to administer in the manner which, in his judgment, is best calculated to produce the most beneficial results for the community—the man of wealth thus becoming the mere agent and trustee of his poorer brethren."
Andrew Carnegie

E. HORATIO ALGER

1. Horatio Alger wrote a series of popular novels that described how impoverished young boys succeeded through hard work, perseverance, and good luck.
2. The novels reinforced the belief that America was a land of opportunity, where self-made men could still earn a fortune.

F. THE KNIGHTS OF LABOR

1. The Knights of Labor was founded in 1869. It adopted an open-membership policy that tried to bring together all workers, including blacks, immigrants, and women, into one large union.
2. Eugene Debs was one of the original founders of the Knights of Labor. Debs advocated government ownership of key industries and natural resources.
3. Membership in the Knights grew rapidly because of a few successful strikes, the growth of the urban population, and the continuing industrialization of the American economy.
4. The Knights' leadership opposed strikes. However, local groups of Knights did call some strikes.
5. It is important to note that the Knights did NOT grow because of federal laws that protected a laborer's right to organize.

G. THE GREAT RAILROAD STRIKE OF 1877

1. The Baltimore and Ohio Railroad's decision to cut wages caused desperate workers to walk off their jobs and go on strike.
2. The first general strike in American history, the Great Railroad Strike of 1877 paralyzed rail service across America for 45 days.
3. The Great Railroad Strike of 1877 did NOT influence the American Federation of Labor. The AFL was founded nine years AFTER the Great Railroad Strike ended.

H. THE HAYMARKET SQUARE RIOT, 1886

1. Labor unions organized a strike at the McCormick reaper factory in Chicago to demand an eight-hour day.
2. On May 4, 1886, nearly 1,500 working people gathered at Chicago's Haymarket Square to protest police actions at the McCormick reaper factory. As the police tried to disperse the crowd, an unidentified person hurled a bomb that killed seven police officers and injured 67 other people.
3. Although no one knew who threw the bomb, the public outcry against unions hastened the decline of the Knights of Labor.

I. SAMUEL GOMPERS AND THE AMERICAN FEDERATION OF LABOR

1. As the Knights of Labor declined, the American Federation of Labor (AFL) began to grow.
2. Led by Samuel Gompers, the AFL organized skilled workers into craft unions.
3. Gompers and the AFL focused on bread-and-butter issues such as wages and working conditions. The AFL did NOT emphasize political issues.
4. Gompers defended the workers' right to strike, saying that it was sometimes a necessary tool to force employers to decrease hours and raise wages.
5. It is interesting to note that middle-class reformers supported the AFL.

J. THE INDUSTRIAL WORKERS OF THE WORLD

1. The AFL's commitment to craft unions excluded many workers. Like the Knights of Labor, the Industrial Workers of the World (or Wobblies) attempted to unite all skilled and unskilled workers.

2. While the AFL focused on "bread and butter" issues, the Industrial Workers of the World was founded on what one of its early leaders called "the irrepressible conflict between the capitalist class and the working class."

3. QUOTE: "The working class and the employing class have nothing in common...It is the historic mission of the working class to do away with the capitalism." Preamble to the IWW Constitution

K. FEDERAL POLICIES TOWARD WORKERS

1. The federal government followed policies that were detrimental to unskilled workers and labor unions.

2. The federal government called out troops to end strikes and followed an open-door immigration policy that allowed cheap laborers to enter the country and compete for jobs.

3. The federal government did NOT promote retirement and workers' compensation programs.

4. The courts used the Sherman Antitrust Act to curb the power of labor unions.

CHAPTER 21
URBAN LIFE AND CULTURE, 1865–1900

A. URBAN GROWTH

1. Between 1870 and 1900, urban centers assumed a dominant role in American life and culture. Just after the Civil War, only one in six Americans lived in a city. By 1900, one in three Americans made their homes in cities.
2. America's rapidly growing cities quickly became centers of both transportation and industry.
3. The expansion of railroad traffic transformed Chicago into America's second-largest city.
4. Refrigerated railroad cars promoted a healthier diet and created a national market for beef. Chicago quickly became a thriving meatpacking center.

B. THE IMPACTOF THE ELECTRIC TROLLEY CAR

1. Richmond, Virginia, successfully tested the first electric trolley system in 1888. Within just two years, 200 other cities opened trolley lines.
2. The new electric street cars encouraged the growth of the central business district.
3. The electric trolley car also promoted the physical expansion of cities. For the first time, employees could commute to work from a new ring of streetcar suburbs.

C. DEPARTMENT STORES AND MAIL-ORDER CATALOGUES

1. Streetcars, electric lights, theaters, and huge new department stores made America's cities exciting places to be.

2. In Chicago, customers flocked to Marshall Field's department store, where they could find an amazing variety of goods under one roof.
3. Marshall Fields and Sears, Roebuck pioneered the development of mail-order catalogues. The catalogues enabled people in isolated rural communities to order goods from big-city department stores.
4. The mail-order catalogues created a national retail market by helping to standardize popular tastes for the same products. The development of national advertising campaigns further accelerated this process.
5. The mail-order catalogues did NOT lead to the decline of traditional big-city department stores. However, they did hurt the business of small-town shopkeepers and merchants.

D. THE NEW IMMIGRANTS

1. Before the 1880s, most immigrants to the United States came from countries in Northern and Western Europe.
2. The last two decades of the 19th century witnessed a massive wave of immigrants from Southern and Eastern Europe. The overwhelming majority of these "new" immigrants came from Italy, Poland, Austro-Hungary, and Russia.
3. The "new" immigrants did NOT come from England or from Scandinavia.

E. NATIVIST REACTION

1. The wave of Irish and German immigrants in the 1840s sparked a NATIVIST, or anti-foreign, reaction among native-born Protestants.
2. The wave of new immigrants from Southern and Eastern Europe provoked an even stronger nativist response.
3. Nativists warned that the new immigrants would not assimilate or become like Americans of earlier times.

F. THE CHINESE EXCLUSION ACT, 1882

1. Although the nativists were unsuccessful in their attempts to restrict immigration from Southern and Eastern Europe, they were able to block Chinese immigration into California and the West Coast.

2. First attracted by the Gold Rush, Chinese immigrants quickly became the largest non-European group living in California.
3. Working-class Californians bitterly complained that Chinese laborers provided unfair competition, because they worked for low wages.
4. Congress responded to the nativist outcry by passing the Chinese Exclusion Act in 1882. The act prohibited Chinese workers from entering the United States.
5. Californians, workers and members of both political parties supported the Chines Exclusion Act.
6. The Chinese Exclusion Act marked America's first law designed to exclude a specific ethnic or race group from immigrating to the United States.

G. BIG CITY POLITICAL MACHINES

1. Tightly organized groups of politicians called machines controlled many big city governments.
2. The machines had a strong centralized organization. Power flowed from a boss down through several levels of command, ending in a ward or neighborhood.
3. Ward politicians like George Washington Plunkett in New York City worked hard to get votes. For example, they helped immigrants settle into cities, providing needy families with baskets of food.
4. QUOTE: "He plays politics every day and night in the year, and his headquarters bears the inscription 'Never Closed.'" George Washington Plunkett, describing the work of an urban political boss
5. Above all, political bosses rewarded loyal followers with government jobs called PATRONAGE. They proudly proclaimed that "to the victors belong the spoils!"
6. QUOTE: "When the people elected Tammany, they knew just what they were doin.' We didn't put up any false pretenses. We didn't go in for humbug civil service and all that rot. We stood as we have always stood, for rewardin' the men that won the victory...When we go in, we fire every anti-Tammany man from office that can be fired under the law." George Washington Plunkett

7. New York City fell under the control of a particularly corrupt machine, led by Boss Tweed. Thomas Nast exposed Tweed's fraudulent practices in a series of political cartoons that mercilessly portrayed the Tweed Ring as a group of thieves and scoundrels.

H. THE SOCIAL GOSPEL

1. Advocates of the Social Gospel believed that American churches had a moral responsibility to take the lead in actively confronting social problems and helping the poor.
2. The Social Gospel movement drew the attention of Protestant churches to the plight of the urban poor.

I. JANE ADDAMS

1. Inspired in part by the Social Gospel movement, Jane Addams dedicated her life to bettering the condition of the urban poor.
2. Addams founded Hull House in Chicago in 1889. Hull House served as a model for the settlement house movement in America.
3. Idealistic middle-class women took the lead in founding over 400 settlement houses in America.
4. Jane Addams did NOT actively work to promote the women's rights movement.

J. REALISTIC ART, LITERATURE, AND PHILOSOPHY

1. The Ashcan School of artists promoted a new artistic realism, by portraying crowded urban tenement buildings, boisterous barrooms, and lively city cafés.
2. Realistic writers, such as Stephen Crane and Theodore Dreiser, wrote novels featuring graphic depictions of people caught in a web of social problems in American cities. It is important to note that that the Realistic movement in literature is sometimes called Naturalism.
3. A new generation of PRAGMATIC philosophers abandoned Transcendentalism in favor of a pragmatic approach that emphasized factual knowledge and practical experience.
4. QUOTE: "The life of the law has not been logic; it has been experience." Oliver Wendell Holmes

CHAPTER 22
THE POPULISTS AND THE PROGRESSIVES, 1880-1920

A. CAUSES OF THE POPULIST REVOLT

1. American farmers had much to complain about during the last two decades of the 19th century.
2. The increased use of machinery transformed American agriculture by enabling farmers to increase the number of acres under cultivation. This in turn enabled farmers to produce more crops. However, as the supply of food increased, farm prices decreased.
3. Angry farmers blamed their worsening economic condition on discriminatory railroad rates, monopoly prices charged for farm machinery, oppressively high tariff rates, and a deflationary monetary policy based on the gold standard.
4. Farm discontent was NOT a response to the free coinage of silver, since the government monetary policy was based upon the gold standard.

B. THE POPULIST PARTY PLATFORM

1. This wave of agrarian anger gave birth to the People's or Populist Party.
2. The major goal of the Populist Party was to unite farmers to improve their economic conditions.
3. The Populist Party platform called for greater government control over the railroads, free coinage of silver, and the direct election of United States senators.
4. It is interesting to note that critics charged that the Populist Party and its platform were an unwieldy collection of splinter parties and impractical ideas.

C. THE INTERSTATE COMMERCE ACT, 1888

1. Congress responded to the public outcry against the railroads by passing the Interstate Commerce Act.
2. The Interstate Commerce Act required the railroads to publish "reasonable and just" rates. It also outlawed secret agreements designed to keep rates high.
3. The Interstate Commerce Act established an important precedent for federal regulation of business and industry.
4. Congress created the Interstate Commerce Commission in 1888 to enforce the new law.
5. Just two years later, Congress passed the Sherman Antitrust Act. It made illegal any sort of combination of businesses that resulted in the "restraint of trade or commerce among the several States."
6. It is important to note that the Interstate Commerce Commission was a regulatory body. In contrast, the Sherman Antitrust Act was created to prohibit specific actions.

D. WILLIAM JENNINGS BRYAN

1. William Jennings Bryan galvanized the 1896 Democratic Party convention with his famous "Cross of Gold" speech, demanding an end to the gold standard and the adoption of free coinage of silver.
2. The Democrats enthusiastically nominated Bryan. He was then endorsed by the Populist Party.
3. William McKinley defeated Bryan in the hotly contested 1896 presidential election. Bryan's defeat led to the collapse of the Populist Party and a new era of Republican Party dominance.

E. *THE WONDERFUL WIZARD OF OZ*

1. L. Frank Baum's *The Wonderful Wizard of Oz* was originally written as a political allegory on free silver and the plight of American farmers.
2. For example, the Scarecrow represents farmers, the Tin Man represents industrial workers, and the Cowardly Lion represents William Jennings Bryan.

F. THE PROGRESSIVE SPIRIT

1. After the collapse of the Populist Party following the 1896 presidential election, the reform spirit shifted to the cities, where a new generation of middle and upper-middle class reformers focused on a broad range of problems caused by industrialization and urbanization.
2. Both the Populists and the Progressives rejected *laissez-faire* government economic policies. Both wanted the government to play an active role in solving social problems.
3. Progressives were often idealists who rejected Social Darwinism. They believed that conflict and competition would NOT inevitably improve society.
4. The Progressive movement dominated American politics until America's entry into World War I diverted public attention to the war effort.

G. MUCKRAKERS AND REFORMERS

1. MUCKRAKERS were Progressive Era journalists who used investigative reporting to expose corrupt practices in business and politics.
2. Upton Sinclair's muckraking novel *The Jungle* exposed unsanitary conditions in the meatpacking industry. His exposé prompted an outraged public to demand that Congress pass the Meat Inspection Act and the Pure Food and Drug Act. This illustrates the relationship between muckraking journalism and reform during the Progressive Era.
3. Ida Tarbell wrote a devastating exposé of the ruthless practices John D. Rockefeller used to eliminate competitors and build the Standard Oil Company into what she called the "Mother of Trusts."
4. Jacob Riis photographed living conditions in crowded tenement buildings in New York City's Lower East Side. His pioneering work helped publicize the poor housing and sanitation in urban tenements.
5. John Dewey was an educational philosopher who believed that children learn best by doing and experimenting.

H. WOMEN AND PROGRESSIVE REFORM

1. When the Progressive Era began, the law denied criminals, lunatics, idiots, and women the right to vote.

2. Opponents of women's suffrage argued that granting women the right to vote would disrupt the natural division of life into separate spheres for family and politics.

3. Proponents of women's suffrage countered by arguing that American life would benefit by spreading women's domestic spirit into the public sphere.

4. Women first obtained the right to vote in Wyoming and other Western states. Despite some progress, women still could NOT vote in all the Western states.

5. Led by Carrie Chapman and Alice Paul, women organized rallies, signed petitions, and demonstrated for the suffrage in public marches. This campaign of public pressure became irresistible. The Nineteenth Amendment formally granted women the right to vote in 1920.

6. Women reformers also played a leading role in the temperance movement to outlaw the sale of alcoholic beverages. The Women's Christian Temperance Union (WCTU) boasted nearly one million members, making it the largest organization of women in the world. The WCTU convinced many women that they had a moral duty to eliminate alcohol and improve society.

7. It is important to note that Betty Friedan did NOT play a role in the Progressive Era fight for women's rights. It is also important to note that Progressive Era women reformers were NOT involved in a fight for an Equal Rights Amendment.

I. THE PROGRESSIVE AMENDMENTS

1. The Sixteenth Amendment gave Congress the power to lay and collect taxes on income. Prior to this amendment, tariffs and land sales constituted the government's primary source of income.

2. The Seventeenth Amendment provided that United States senators would be elected by popular vote.

3. The Eighteenth Amendment forbade the sale or manufacture of intoxicating liquors.

4. The Nineteenth Amendment granted women the right to vote.

5. The Progressive Era constitutional amendments did NOT include a law banning child labor. Progressive reformers did succeed in passing child labor laws at the state level.

J. THEODORE ROOSEVELT, 1901–1909

1. TR was known as a "trust buster" because he launched antitrust action against the Northern Securities Company. TR believed that he had a duty to regulate trusts that did NOT benefit society as a whole.
2. TR secured passage of the Hepburn Act to regulate the railroads.
3. TR intervened in the 1902 United Mine Workers' strike by forcing mine owners to accept federal arbitration.
4. TR supported the conservation movement by adding millions of acres to the national park system.
5. TR did NOT actively promote civil rights legislation. He did reach out to African Americans by inviting Booker T. Washington to dine with him in the White House.
6. TR did NOT address the issue of insider trading on the stock market.
7. TR did NOT ask Congress to consider a constitutional amendment granting women the right to vote.
8. TR founded the new Progressive or Bull Moose Party to advance his political comeback and promote Progressive reforms. The party split the Republican vote and played a key role in enabling the Democrats, led by Woodrow Wilson, to win the 1912 presidential election.

K. WOODROW WILSON, 1913–1921

1. Like TR, Woodrow Wilson sought to limit corporations that had become too large and powerful.
2. Wilson supported the Nineteenth Amendment, which granted women the right to vote.

L. AFRICAN AMERICANS DURING THE PROGRESSIVE ERA

1. Progressive Era reformers were LEAST concerned with promoting civil rights legislation and ending racial segregation.
2. The Progressives did NOT work for laws banning the poll tax or literacy tests.
3. W.E.B. Du Bois favored full economic, social, and political integration for African Americans.
4. Du Bois and other black and white reformers founded the National Association for the Advancement of Colored People (NAACP) in 1909. The NAACP was committed to using the courts to strike down Jim Crow segregation laws.
5. Ida B. Wells was an African American who became the principal public opponent of lynching in the United States.

M. THE ARTS AND POPULAR CULTURE

1. The 1913 Armory Show in New York City exposed Americans to the Cubist paintings of Picasso and other modern masters.
2. The rapid growth of cities helped stimulate the growing popularity of Major League Baseball.
3. Scott Joplin was an important African American composer who helped to popularize Ragtime music. Ragtime fell out of favor as jazz claimed the public imagination during the Roaring Twenties.

CHAPTER 23
IMPERIALISM AND THE FIRST WORLD WAR, 1890-1919

A. THE ROOTS OF EXPANSIONISM

1. In 1890, the United States still played a minor role in the global game of power politics. Then in less than a decade America became an imperial republic with interests in the Caribbean, Latin America, and the Pacific.

2. Business leaders worried that their factories were producing more goods than Americans could buy. Many corporate executives looked to Latin America, Asia, and the Pacific for new markets and new sources of raw materials.

3. Captain Alfred T. Mahan published *The Influence of Sea Power upon History* in 1890. Mahan's book played an influential role in shaping late 19th-century American policy toward the importance of naval power.

4. Theodore Roosevelt, Senator Henry Cabot Lodge, and Alfred Mahan were all influential expansionists who argued that the United States must build a strong navy, construct a canal through Central America, acquire fueling stations in the Pacific, and gain possessions in the Caribbean. They did NOT favor acquiring Alaska, since this territory had already been purchased from Russia in 1867.

5. Other expansionists argued that America had a responsibility to spread Christianity to Asia.

6. It is interesting to note that acquiring territories for America's excess population was the LEAST used argument for expansion.

7. QUOTE: "If the Democratic Party has had one cardinal principle beyond all others, it has been that of pushing forward the boundaries of the United States. Under this administration, this

great principle has been utterly abandoned...Mr. Cleveland has labored to overthrow American interests and American control in Hawaii. Andrew Jackson fought for Florida but Mr. Cleveland is eager to abandon Samoa." Senator Henry Cabot Lodge, expressing his conviction that the United States had to follow an expansionist policy

8. QUOTE: "God has not been preparing the English-speaking and Teutonic people for a thousand years for nothing but vain and idle self-contemplation and self-admiration. No! He has made us the Master organizers of the world to establish system where chaos reigns. He has given us the spirit of progress to overwhelm the forces of reaction throughout the earth...And of all our race He has marked the American people as His chosen nation to finally lead in the regeneration of the world." Senator Albert J. Beveridge, expressing his support for U.S. imperialism

B. THE OPEN DOOR POLICY, 1899

1. American business leaders looked to China's vast market to spur economic growth.
2. During the 1880s and 1890s Great Britain, Germany, France, Russia, and Japan all carved out spheres of influence in an ever-weakening China.
3. Secretary of State John Hay sent Open Door notes to all of the nations involved in China. Hay formally requested that these nations agree to respect the rights and privileges of other nations within their respective spheres of influence.
4. It is important to remember that the Open Door policy was designed to protect American commercial interests in China.

C. CAUSES OF THE SPANISH-AMERICAN WAR

1. William Randolph Hearst's New York Journal and Joseph Pulitzer's New York World were locked in a furious circulation war for readers. Both papers published daily stories about Spanish atrocities in Cuba. Known as "yellow journalism," these sensational stories sparked widespread public indignation against Spain.

2. On February 15, 1898, the 7,000-ton U.S.S. *Maine*, the navy's newest battleship, mysteriously exploded in Havana Harbor. Although the cause of the blast has never been fully determined, the press and most Americans blamed the Spanish.

3. America's Catholic heritage was NOT a factor in causing the Spanish-American War.

4. After some hesitation, President McKinley announced his decision to use force to liberate Cuba from Spanish oppression. Congress declared war on Spain on April 25, 1898.

D. CONSEQUENCES OF THE SPANISH-AMERICAN WAR

1. The Spanish-American War lasted just 114 days. It is often called a "splendid little war" because America quickly defeated Spain and achieved its goals in both Cuba and the Philippines.

2. The Spanish-American War marked the emergence of the United States as a world power.

3. The Treaty of Paris ceded Puerto Rico and Guam to the United States. Spain recognized Cuban independence and agreed to cede the Philippine Islands to the United States for $20 million. This marked the first time that the United States acquired overseas territory.

4. It is important to note that the United States acquired Puerto Rico and the Philippines by force and not by negotiation.

E. THE DEBATE OVER THE PHILIPPINES

1. In February 1899, the British novelist and poet Rudyard Kipling wrote a poem entitled "The White Man's Burden: The United States and the Philippine Islands." In his poem, Kipling urged America to take up "the burden" of bringing the blessings of Western civilization to the Philippines. While Theodore Roosevelt and other expansionists agreed with Kipling, anti-imperialists viewed the phrase "White Man's burden" as a euphemism for imperialism.

2. The provision in the Treaty of Paris of 1898 ceding the Philippines to the United States aroused a strong anti-imperialist movement to block ratification of the treaty.

3. The Anti-Imperialist League argued that controlling the Philippines would be contrary to America's long-standing commitment to human freedom and rule by the "consent of the people."
4. After a heated debate, the Senate approved the Treaty of Paris by just one vote.
5. Despite strong evidence that the Filipinos wanted independence, the McKinley administration decided that they were not ready for self-government.
6. Led by Emilio Aquinaldo, the Filipinos waged a costly guerrilla war that required three years of brutal fighting to suppress.
7. It is important to note that the United States granted the Philippines its independence immediately following the Second World War.

F. THE PANAMA CANAL

1. Theodore Roosevelt's acquisition of the Canal Zone in Panama illustrates his use of "big stick" diplomacy.
2. TR secured America's exclusive right to construct and control the Panama Canal.
3. The Panama Canal reduced the voyage from San Francisco to the Caribbean from 12,000 miles to 4,000 miles.

G. THE ROOSEVELT COROLLARY

1. The construction of the Panama Canal made the security of the Caribbean a vital American interest.
2. The Monroe Doctrine stated America's opposition to European intervention in the Western Hemisphere. TR updated the Monroe Doctrine by declaring that "flagrant cases of wrongdoing" in Central America and the Caribbean "may force the United States to exercise an international police power."
3. The Roosevelt Corollary, like the Monroe Doctrine, was a unilateral declaration. It modified the Monroe Doctrine from a statement against the intervention of European powers in the affairs of the Western Hemisphere to a policy proclaiming a policing role for the United States in Caribbean affairs.

4. QUOTE: "Chronic wrongdoing, or an impotence which results in a general loosening of the ties of civilized society, may in America, as elsewhere, ultimately require intervention by some civilized nation, and in the Western Hemisphere the adherence of the United States to the Monroe Doctrine may force the United States...to the exercise of an international police power." Theodore Roosevelt

5. TR first applied the Roosevelt Corollary when America assumed responsibility for customs house collections in the Dominican Republic.

H. TAFT AND DOLLAR DIPLOMACY

1. Instead of applying TR's big stick diplomacy, President Taft preferred a policy that many called DOLLAR DIPLOMACY. That is, he used American money to influence the foreign policy of other countries.

2. Taft's use of American bankers to refinance the foreign debt of Nicaragua provides an example of Dollar Diplomacy in action.

I. WILSON AND MEXICAN-AMERICAN RELATIONS

1. Pancho Villa was a Mexican leader who felt betrayed by Wilson's decision to support one of his political rivals.

2. Villa and his men retaliated by stopping a train in northern Mexico and killing 17 American citizens. Two months later, Villa and a band of armed men crossed the border and set fire to the town of Columbus, New Mexico.

3. Outraged by Villa's hostile actions, President Wilson ordered a force of 11,000 men, commanded by General Pershing, to invade Mexico and capture Villa.

4. Pershing failed to capture Villa, and the invasion damaged relations between the U.S. and Mexico.

J. THE ROAD TO WAR

1. President Wilson attempted to keep America out of the First World War while at the same time insisting on American neutral rights on the high seas.

2. On May 7, 1915, a German submarine sank the *Lusitania*, a British passenger liner. Almost 1,200 people died, including 128 Americans. The sinking of the *Lusitania* forcibly raised the issue of freedom of the seas while also raising the issue of American military preparedness.

3. In February 1917 the British intercepted a telegram from the German Foreign Secretary Arthur Zimmerman, addressed to the German minister in Mexico. The note tried to rekindle Mexican resentment over the loss of its territory to the United States in the Mexican-American War. Germany offered to help Mexico regain its "lost territories in New Mexico, Texas, and Arizona." The Zimmerman Note increased tensions between the United States and Germany.

4. The United States entered the First World War on April 2, 1917, as a direct result of Germany's resumption of unrestricted submarine warfare.

5. The United States fought against a coalition of Central Powers that included Germany, Austria-Hungary, the Ottoman Empire, and Bulgaria.

K. THE HOMEFRONT

1. The Great Migration of African Americans from the South to the North began during the First World War. African Americans were attracted by the demand for labor in Northern factories. However, AFL recruiters did NOT persuade African Americans to leave the South.

2. The First World War diverted public attention to foreign affairs. As a result, the era of Progressive reforms came to an end.

3. Recruiting posters often used portraits of women to encourage male volunteers to join the Navy. However, the posters did NOT encourage women to join the armed forces.

4. Led by George Creel, the Committee of Public Information mobilized public opinion to support the war effort.

5. The government financed the war by selling war bonds and by raising tax rates on individuals and estates.

6. The Supreme Court did NOT render wartime decisions that supported individual liberties.

L. THE FOURTEEN POINTS

1. Wilson's Fourteen Points included open diplomacy, freedom of the seas, partial disarmament, and self-determination of peoples. It is important to remember that self-determination was a key principle that underlay many of Wilson's points.
2. Wilson's Fourteenth Point called for the creation of a League of Nations.
3. The Fourteen Points did NOT include creating an International Monetary Fund, maintaining secret alliances, recognizing the Soviet Union, creating a global currency, or recognizing the right to individualism.

M. THE TREATY OF VERSAILLES

1. Securing a charter for the League of Nations was one of Wilson's primary goals at the Versailles conference.
2. The Versailles Treaty did NOT include either provisions for arms reductions or a call for a global currency.
3. Senate opponents, led by Henry Cabot Lodge, argued that the League of Nations would limit American sovereignty and violate Washington's Farewell Address by involving the United States in entangling foreign alliances.
4. Wilson tried to influence the Senate by embarking on a grueling cross-country speaking tour. However, he collapsed from exhaustion and then suffered a severe stroke that partly paralyzed the left side of his body.
5. The Senate never approved the Treaty of Versailles, and the United States never joined the League of Nations.

CHAPTER 24
THE ROARING TWENTIES, 1919–1929

A. THE RED SCARE AND INTOLERANCE

1. In 1917 the Communist Party, led by Vladimir Lenin, successfully established a Communist dictatorship in Russia. Developments in Russia frightened many Americans and sparked a widespread fear of Communists and aliens that is called the RED SCARE.

2. Attorney General A. Mitchell Palmer feared and hated Communists and radicals. In early January 1920, he ordered a series of raids, called Palmer raids, to arrest foreign-born radicals.

3. The Red Scare reached new heights with the arrest and execution of Nicola Sacco and Bartolomeo Vanzetti. Both men were Italian immigrants and avowed anarchists, accused of robbing and killing a paymaster in South Braintree, Massachusetts. The Sacco and Vanzetti case underscored the nation's fear of radicals and recent immigrants.

4. Businesses used the Red Scare to discourage workers from forming and joining unions.

B. NATIVISM AND IMMIGRATION RESTRICTION

1. The Red Scare fueled increased public support for laws to limit immigration from Southern and Eastern Europe.

2. The National Origins Act of 1924 established quotas based on a percentage of each national group residing in the United States in 1890. Since the wave of immigration from Southern and Eastern Europe took place after 1890, the quotas intentionally discriminated against these groups.

3. The National Origins Act dramatically restricted the flow of immigrants from Southern and Eastern Europe. For example, the quota allowed 65,361 people to immigrate from Great Britain and just 5,802 from Italy.

C. THE SCOPES TRIAL

1. In January 1925 the state of Tennessee passed the Butler Act, forbidding the teaching of evolution in the state's public schools.
2. Later that year, John T. Scopes, a Tennessee high school science teacher, was arrested for teaching his students about evolution.
3. Clarence Darrow, a well-known champion of civil liberties, agreed to defend Scopes. William Jennings Bryan, a three-time Democratic presidential candidate and a well-known fundamentalist, represented the state of Tennessee.
4. The Scopes Trial ostensibly tested the legality of teaching the theory of evolution in Tennessee's public schools. However, for a national and international audience the case illustrated a growing cultural conflict between fundamentalism, represented by Bryan, and modernism, represented by Darrow.
5. It is important to remember that fundamentalism was both anti-liberal and anti-foreign.

D. THE REVIVAL OF THE KU KLUX KLAN

1. The first half of the 1920s witnessed an alarming rebirth of the Ku Klux Klan. Klan membership peaked at around four million in 1924.
2. D.W. Griffith's epic film *The Birth of a Nation* played a key role by depicting the KKK as a commendable and even heroic organization.
3. During the 1920s, the KKK was both anti-Black and anti-immigrant.
4. Klan membership began to decline following the passage of the National Origins Act of 1924.
5. The revival of the KKK and the National Origins Act both illustrate intolerance and nativism during the 1920s. However, the Teapot Dome scandal was NOT an example of either nativism or intolerance.

E. THE GREAT MIGRATION CONTINUES

1. The Great Migration of African Americans from the rural South to industrial cities in the North and West began during the First World War.
2. The Great Migration continued during the 1920s. By 1930, another 600,000 African Americans had moved to cities in the North.

F. THE HARLEM RENAISSANCE

1. Harlem soon emerged as a vibrant center of African American culture.
2. During the 1920s, a new generation of African American writers and artists created an outpouring of literature and culture known as the HARLEM RENAISSANCE.
3. Langston Hughes, Jean Toomer, James Weldon Jones, Claude McKay, and Zora Neale Hurston formed the core group of Harlem Renaissance writers. They all believed that African Americans should take pride in their culture and accomplishments.
4. It is important to note that A. Philip Randolph was an African American civil rights leader who was NOT a member of the Harlem Renaissance.
5. Claude McKay was an outspoken advocate of the New Negro concept. McKay and others called for African Americans to shed their old image of inferiority and adopt a new sense of racial pride.

G. MARCUS GARVEY

1. Marcus Garvey emerged as one of the earliest and most influential black-nationalist leaders in the 20th century.
2. Garvey emphasized the importance of Black pride and Pan-Africanism.
3. Garvey founded the Universal Negro Improvement Association. He was NOT a member of the Student Nonviolent Coordinating Committee (SNCC).

H. THE JAZZ AGE

1. Jazz emerged as the music most identified with the Roaring Twenties.
2. Jazz was especially popular in urban areas.

3. For many of its fans, jazz represented a break with traditional music.
4. European music critics viewed jazz as the first truly American art.
5. Billie Holliday was one of the era's most popular jazz singers.
6. "Duke" Ellington was a well-known African American composer, pianist, and big band leader who began his career in Harlem.
7. Although the 1920s are often called the Jazz Age, it is important to remember that motion pictures, or movies, were the era's most popular form of entertainment. By the end of the decade as many as 80 million Americans watched a movie in one of America's 20,000 theaters.

I. THE NEW WOMAN

1. The new independent spirit symbolized by jazz also expressed itself in the changes many postwar women were making in their lives.
2. Although most women still worked as domestic servants, sales clerks, garment workers, and teachers, a vanguard of college-educated women sought new careers in law, medicine, and science.
3. Young "modern women," called FLAPPERS, challenged traditional codes of dress and behavior.
4. Margaret Sanger was a leading feminist who advocated birth control.

J. PROHIBITION

1. Supporters of the Eighteenth Amendment hoped that prohibition would reduce crime and improve family life.
2. Instead, prohibition generated a booming illegal business in the sale and distribution of alcoholic beverages. Ironically, prohibition promoted the growth of organized crime.
3. It is important to remember that prohibition received its greatest support from white Protestants.
4. Prohibition failed because alcoholic consumption was a deeply ingrained part of American popular culture.
5. It is interesting to note that prohibition did NOT affect the supply of medicinal alcohol.

K. THE LOST GENERATION WRITERS

1. F. Scott Fitzgerald, Sinclair Lewis, and Ernest Hemingway wrote about their disillusionment with American materialism and conformity. They were known as the LOST GENERATION writers because many were expatriates who chose to leave the United States and live in Paris.
2. Sinclair Lewis satirized middle-class life in his novel *Main Street*.
3. Written by Ernest Hemingway, *A Farewell to Arms* was a novel set during World War I. It was NOT a novel about life during Reconstruction.
4. Hemingway's novel *The Sun Also Rises* captured the Lost Generation's strength and resilience. The novel was NOT about the Baby Boom generation.

L. FROM HARDING TO HOOVER

1. The Republican Party won all three presidential elections held during the 1920s.
2. Presidents Harding, Coolidge, and Hoover all supported a close partnership between government and business. After winning the 1924 election, Coolidge confidently asserted that "the business of America is business."
3. All three Republican administrations reduced taxes for the wealthy, raised tariffs, and ignored anti-trust legislation.
4. President Coolidge recognized that American society was economically stratified. However, he also believed that American society was fundamentally harmonious. He called for economic legislation that would lower taxes and "create conditions in which everyone will have a better chance to be successful."

M. FOREIGN POLICY

1. President Harding hosted a Washington disarmament conference to place limits on the expensive arms race among the great powers.
2. The conference members agreed to create ratios for the construction of new warships. For example, American and Britain enjoyed parity in battleships and aircraft carriers, with Japan on the short end of a 5:5:3 ratio.

3. The United States responded to the German economic crisis by adopting the Dawes Plan to provide loans to help alleviate German war debts.

N. MASS PRODUCTION AND MASS CONSUMPTION

1. The 1920s witnessed the mass production of a new generation of affordable consumer products, such as refrigerators, washing machines, electric irons, and vacuum cleaners.
2. The mass production of automobiles had the greatest impact upon American life. Henry Ford successfully applied the principle of moving assembly line production to the manufacture of automobiles. By 1925, the Ford Motor Company produced a new car every ten seconds.
3. Although the Ford Motor Company did produce affordable cars, it did NOT make a variety of products. Until the debut of the Model A in 1927, all Model T cars were black.
4. The 1920s witnessed an increase in the number of men and women working in office jobs.
5. The dramatic increase in American production raised living standards during the 1920s. Most Americans agreed with President Hoover when he confidently predicted, "We in America are nearer to the final triumph over poverty than ever before in the history of any land."

CHAPTER 25
THE GREAT DEPRESSION AND THE NEW DEAL, 1929-1941

A. CAUSES OF THE GREAT DEPRESSION

1. Farmers in the Midwest and South did NOT share in the good times of of the 1920s. The global surplus of agricultural products drove prices, and thus farm incomes, down. It is important to remember that overproduction had been the biggest problem for farmers since the 1880s.

2. The United States economy was simultaneously experiencing overproduction by business and underconsumption by consumers. By the summer of 1929, many businesses had large inventories of unsold goods. Many factory workers lost their jobs as industries cut back production because of falling demand for their products.

3. Stock prices began to fall in September 1929. In late October they crashed, as stocks lost 37 percent of their value in just one week.

4. The Great Depression was NOT caused by excessive government regulation.

5. The Great Depression was NOT a period of inflation. It was a period of falling prices or deflation.

B. THE GREAT DEPRESSION DEEPENS

1. The stock market crash triggered a steep decline in industrial production.

2. As more and more companies shut their doors, the unemployment rate sharply rose. By 1932, a quarter of all American workers had lost their jobs.

3. Prolonged unemployment created an army of transient people looking for work.

4. HOOVERVILLE was the sarcastic term given to shanty towns inhabited by unemployed and homeless people.
5. The lyrics of this 1930s song capture Americans sense of despair during the depths of the Great Depression:
"Once I built a railroad, made it run,
Made it race against time.
Once I built a railroad, now it's done.
Brother can you spare a dime?"

C. THE DUST BOWL

1. A severe drought hit the Great Plains starting in 1930. The lack of rain combined with unusually hot summers created great clouds of dust out of what had once been fertile soil.
2. Large areas of Oklahoma, Kansas, and Colorado became known as the Dust Bowl.
3. Alexandre Hogue's painting "Drought Stricken Area" depicts a barren windswept landscape and a devastated farm in the heart of the Dust Bowl.
4. Called Okies, over 350,000 desperate people fled the Great Plains during the 1930s. John Steinbeck captured the ordeal faced by these proud but impoverished migrants in his powerful novel, *The Grapes of Wrath*.
5. Dorothea Lange was a photographer whose poignant pictures publicized the plight of migrant farm workers and their families.

D. HERBERT HOOVER AND THE GREAT DEPRESSION

1. President Hoover believed that the economy was basically sound and that recovery depended upon the support of the business community.
2. Hoover did NOT support federal programs to aid unemployed workers. However, he did support federal loans to private businesses and to state governments.
3. Hoover established the Reconstruction Finance Corporation (RFC) in a belated attempt to fight the Great Depression. The RFC provided federal loans to banks and private businesses.
4. Hoover's sinking popularity fell even further because of his handling of an event called the Bonus March.

5. In the spring of 1932, some 20,000 World War I veterans converged on Washington, D.C., to lobby Congress to pass a bill providing the immediate payment of their promised wartime bonuses.

6. Supported by Hoover, the Senate rejected the bill. Despite this defeat, many veterans and their families encamped in Washington. Upset by the presence of so many unemployed men in the nation's capital, Hoover ordered the army to forcibly remove the Bonus Marchers.

7. The Bonus Army resembled Coxey's Army in 1894. Both marches occurred during periods of economic depression, and both groups demanded immediate economic relief.

E. FDR AND THE NEW DEAL

1. The deepening depression crippled any chance Hoover had of winning reelection. Sensing victory, the Democrats nominated Franklin D. Roosevelt, the popular reform-minded governor of New York. FDR won an overwhelming victory, ushering in a period of Democratic political dominance that lasted for 20 years.

2. During the 1932 presidential campaign, FDR promised "a new deal for the American people." It is important to remember that FDR was a pragmatist who was willing to experiment. The New Deal sought to restructure American capitalism, not replace it. The New Deal was thus a program of reform and not revolution.

3. The New Deal launched a massive spending program to jumpstart the economy.

4. FDR used DEFICIT SPENDING to finance the New Deal programs. Recommended by the British economist John Maynard Keynes, deficit spending means that the government spends more money than it takes in.

5. The New Deal included programs designed for both short-term recovery and long-term reform.

6. The Civilian Conservation Corps (CCC) combined jobs for unemployed youth with projects designed to restore the environment.

7. The Agricultural Adjustment Act (AAA) attempted to reduce farm surpluses by decreasing the amount of land under cultivation. Supporters of the law believed that this would raise crop prices and thus ensure farmers an adequate standard of living.

8. Congress created the Securities Exchange Commission (SEC) to regulate the stock market.

9. The Tennessee Valley Authority (TVA) was a long-term program that built dams designed to provide cheap electricity, prevent floods, and serve as a model of regional planning.

10. The Works Projects Administration (WPA) helped relieve unemployment by providing jobs for out-of-work artists and writers.

11. The National Recovery Act (NRA) allowed businesses to regulate themselves through codes of fair competition. The symbol of the NRA was a Blue Eagle insignia. It became a prominent feature in political cartoons in the early 1930s.

12. The Indian Reorganization Act of 1934 reversed the Dawes Plan by stopping the sale of Indian tribal lands.

13. The Twenty-First Amendment repealed the Eighteenth Amendment, thus restoring the right to legally purchase alcoholic beverages.

14. The Social Security Act guaranteed retirement payments to enrolled workers beginning at the age of 65. The act was influenced by earlier proposals advocated by Dr. Francis Townsend. Social Security proved to be the most far-reaching New Deal program.

15. The New Deal did NOT nationalize the banks, restructure the courts, establish the Lend-Lease program or attempt to replace America's capitalist system.

16. The New Deal DID have critics. For example, Father Coughlin was a popular "Radio Priest" who wanted FDR to nationalize the banks and coin more silver dollars.

F. THE NEW DEAL AND LABOR

1. When the Great Depression began, trade unions represented only about three million workers. Most were skilled workers organized by the American Federation of Labor (AFL).
2. The Wagner Act (National Labor Relations Act) guaranteed every laborer the right to join a union and use the union to bargain collectively.
3. John L. Lewis, the leader of the United Mine Workers, took the lead in forming the Congress of Industrial Organizations (CIO) to unionize unskilled and semi-skilled workers within a single industry.
4. The CIO welcomed unskilled workers, women, and African Americans into its ranks.
5. American unions and their members benefitted from the New Deal. By the end of the 1930s, unions represented nine million workers, or 28 percent of the non-farm work force.

G. THE NEW DEAL AND AFRICAN AMERICANS

1. Although the New Deal did NOT directly confront racial injustice, African Americans did benefit from some New Deal programs.
2. During the 1930s, large numbers of African American voters switched their allegiance from the Republican to the Democratic Party.
3. African Americans became an important part of a New Deal coalition of voters that included organized labor, urban residents, ethnic minorities, and white southerners. The New Deal coalition did NOT include industrialists.

H. THE NEW DEAL AND WOMEN

1. The New Deal did not directly challenge gender inequity.
2. Eleanor Roosevelt was the most visible champion of women's rights during the New Deal era.

I. THE NEW DEAL AND THE SUPREME COURT

1. The Supreme Court stunned FDR and his New Deal supporters by striking down the National Recovery Act (NRA) and the Agricultural Adjustment Act (AAA).
2. FDR feared that the Court would soon strike down the Wagner Act and the Social Security Act.
3. In 1937, FDR sent Congress a plan to increase the number of justices on the Supreme Court.
4. Both the public and members of Congress opposed FDR's "court-packing" plan as a violation of judicial independence and the separation of powers.
5. The Supreme Court proved to be more sympathetic to the New Deal after FDR's court-packing fiasco. The Court upheld both the Wagner Act and the Social Security Act.

J. THE NEW DEAL AND THE DEPRESSION

1. The New Deal did NOT end the Great Depression.
2. Massive military spending at the start of World War II created an economic boom that ended the Great Depression.

CHAPTER 26
THE SECOND WORLD WAR, 1931-1945

A. ISOLATIONISM AND THE NEUTRALITY ACTS

1. In the years following the First World War, American ISOLATIONISTS argued that the United States should avoid entangling alliances with other countries. They urged their fellow countrymen to remember George Washington's Farewell Address admonition to avoid being involved in European affairs.

2. In 1934, Senator Gerald P. Nye chaired a special Senate committee that investigated how and why the United States became involved in World War I. The Nye Committee concluded that greedy companies they branded as "merchants of death" lured America into the war. These corporations then proceeded to make enormous wartime profits.

3. Prompted by the Nye Committee's revelations, Congress passed a series of Neutrality Acts. Isolationists were convinced that these laws would keep the United States out of a new war.

B. TOWARD AMERICAN INVOLVEMENT

1. While the Isolationists tried to keep America out of a new war, events in Asia and Europe drew the United States ever closer to entering the Second World War.

2. In 1931, Japan broke several treaty pledges by invading China's northern province of Manchuria. Secretary of State Henry Stimson responded by declaring a policy of nonrecognition, called the Stimson Doctrine. The Japanese ignored the toothless Stimson Doctrine and quickly incorporated Manchuria into their rapidly expanding empire.

3. In 1933, FDR opened a new chapter in America's relationship with Latin America by proclaiming the beginning of a GOOD NEIGHBOR POLICY. The new policy renounced the Roosevelt Corollary and created reciprocal trade agreements between the United States and several Latin American countries. During the 1930s, the Good Neighbor Policy promoted a common hemispheric front against fascism.

4. Mussolini tested the League of Nations system of collective security by invading Ethiopia. The League's failure to act inspired Hitler to defy the Versailles Treaty by entering the Rhineland and then annexing Austria and a portion of western Czechoslovakia, called the Sudetenland.

5. On September 1, 1939, Hitler launched a sudden massive blitzkrieg, or "lightening war," against Poland. France and Great Britain immediately declared war on Germany.

6. The frightening events in Europe persuaded many Americans to support rebuilding the nation's military strength. However, a majority of the American public still wanted to remain neutral.

7. Aware of the danger posed by Hitler's conquest of Poland and Western Europe, FDR began a Cash and Carry program of sending surplus military equipment to Great Britain.

8. In a fireside chat on December 29, 1940, FDR explained that America must become an "arsenal of democracy" by providing additional war supplies to Great Britain.

9. Congress passed the Lend-Lease Act in March 1941. Under the Lend-Lease program, the United States supplied Great Britain, the Soviet Union and other Allied nations with vast amounts of military equipment. It is important to note that the Lend-Lease Act was NOT part of the New Deal.

10. Lend-Lease and the Atlantic Charter were both designed to show support for Great Britain.

C. PEARL HARBOR

1. The war in Europe overshadowed ominous problems between the United States and Japan.

2. Tension between the two Pacific powers escalated when Japanese forces overran French Indochina in July 1941. FDR retaliated by ordering a total embargo of oil and scrap iron shipments to Japan.

3. When negotiations with Japan reached an impasse, the Japanese launched a surprise attack on the American fleet stationed at Pearl Harbor.
4. The sneak attack on Pearl Harbor ended American neutrality. An angry and united America now entered World War II determined to crush Japan and Germany.

D. WARTIME DIPLOMACY

1. Outraged Americans demanded a strategy designed to first defeat Japan and then crush Germany. However, FDR realized that Hitler posed the greatest threat to America's long-term security. The United States and Great Britain therefore agreed upon a military strategy of defeating Hitler first.
2. During the Second World War, the Big Three referred to FDR, Churchill, and the Soviet leader Joseph Stalin.
3. At a meeting held in Tehran, Iran, the Big Three agreed to demand the unconditional surrender of both Germany and Italy.
4. Upon becoming President in April 1945, Harry S. Truman appointed James B. Byrne as his new Secretary of State. Byrne played a key role in helping Truman negotiate the end of the war. Byrne's diplomatic papers thus form a valuable resource for students studying the diplomatic history of World War II.
5. It is important to remember that the United States and the Soviet Union were allies during World War II. The United States therefore did NOT deport Russians during the war.

E. AFRICAN AMERICANS AND WORLD WAR II

1. The Second World War created expanded job opportunities in the North and West. As a result, the Great Migration of African Americans out of the South continued.
2. About one million African Americans served in the armed forces during World War II. These black soldiers and sailors continued to serve in segregated units.
3. African Americans were keenly aware of the contradiction between fighting for democracy abroad while enduring racial discrimination at home. African Americans enthusiastically supported a "Double V" campaign to win victory over fascism in Europe and discrimination in the United States.
4. American propaganda posters tried to divert attention from racial divisions by stressing the theme of "United We Win!"

F. ROSIE THE RIVETER

1. World War II created expanded job opportunities for American women to work at well-paying jobs formerly performed by men.
2. Rosie the Riveter was a fictional character who became a popular symbol of working women during the Second World War.
3. Eleanor Roosevelt continued to be a leading proponent of women's rights.

G. THE ZOOT SUIT RIOTS

1. Young Mexican Americans in Los Angeles enjoyed a youth culture that included a distinctive "zoot suit" that featured a long coat and baggy trousers.
2. Soldiers and sailors stationed in Los Angeles accused the Mexican American teens of being unpatriotic by deliberately flouting wartime restrictions on the use of fabrics. In 1943, a series of incidents between young Mexican Americans and off-duty servicemen escalated into "Zoot Suit" riots that lasted a week.

H. THE INTERNMENT OF JAPANESE AMERICANS

1. In the days and weeks following the attack on Pearl Harbor, frightened Americans displaced their rage against Japan to the 110,000 people of Japanese birth and descent living on the West Coast.
2. The War Relocation Authority relocated Japanese Americans to ten detention camps, located on desolate lands owned by the federal government.
3. The internment of Japanese Americans raised serious constitutional questions concerning the inalienable rights of American citizens during a war.
4. In *Korematsu v. United States*, the Supreme Court upheld the constitutionality of the government's evacuation policy, citing the existence of "the gravest imminent danger to public safety."
5. The Japanese internment is now recognized as the most serious violation of civil liberties in wartime in American history.

I. THE ATOMIC BOMB

1. FDR approved the $2 billion top secret Manhattan Project to build an atomic bomb.

2. The United States successfully tested an atomic bomb at a desolate stretch of desert in New Mexico on July 16, 1945. At that time, the United States had just two atomic bombs in its arsenal.

3. President Truman authorized the use of atomic bombs on the Japanese cities of Hiroshima and Nagasaki.

4. Truman was motivated by a variety of factors. He wanted to shock Japan into surrendering, thus saving the lives of American soldiers preparing to invade the Japanese home islands. He may also have been motivated by a desire to quickly end the war against Japan, thus detering Soviet expansion in Asia. And finally, Truman may have wanted to convince Stalin of the need to be more cooperative in formulating postwar plans for Germany.

5. Truman's decision to use the atomic bomb was NOT influenced by public opinion, since the bomb's existence was a top secret.

6. Truman's decision to use the atomic bomb against Japan had nothing to do with Germany. It is important to remember that Germany had already surrendered.

CHAPTER 27
TRUMAN AND THE COLD WAR, 1945-1952

A. WINSTON CHURCHILL AND THE IRON CURTAIN SPEECH

1. Following World War II, the Soviet Union steadily tightened its grip on Eastern Europe. In a famous speech given in Fulton, Missouri, Winston Churchill warned that the Soviet Union was rapidly creating a sphere of influence in Eastern Europe.

2. Churchill warned that the nations of Eastern Europe were rapidly disappearing behind an "iron curtain" of secrecy and isolation, imposed by the Soviet leader Joseph Stalin.

3. QUOTE: "A shadow has fallen upon the scenes so lately lighted by the Allied victory. From Stettin in the Baltic to Trieste in the Adriatic an Iron Curtain has descended across the Continent."

4. Each report about the loss of freedom in Eastern Europe substantiated Churchill's warning and increased tensions between the United States and the Soviet Union.

B. THE TRUMAN DOCTRINE AND CONTAINMENT

1. George Kennan was one of America's foremost experts on the Soviet Union. Kennan believed that Soviet hostility would continue for many years to come. In an influential "long telegram," he recommended that the United States should counter Soviet pressure by adopting a policy of "long-term, patient but firm and vigilant containment." By CONTAINMENT, Kennan meant adopting a strategic policy of blocking the expansion of Soviet influence.

2. Truman agreed with both Kennan's analysis and his policy recommendation. He recognized that the Soviet Union's large military presence in Eastern Europe was a potent asset that represented a threat to Western Europe.

3. QUOTE: "It must be the policy of the United States to support free peoples who are resisting attempted subjugations by armed minorities or by outside pressures. I believe that we must assist free peoples to work out their own destinies in their own way."

4. As the leader of the free world, Truman pledged to use America's strength to limit the spread of Communism throughout the world. This pledge became known as the Truman Doctrine.

5. The threat of Communist expansion was not limited to Eastern Europe. Soviet pressure threatened the independence of Greece and Turkey. Truman promptly sent economic aid to both countries. This marked the first use of the Truman Doctrine. It is important to note that the United States did not send nuclear weapons to Greece or to Turkey.

C. The Marshall Plan

1. Greece and Turkey were not the only countries that needed aid. World War II left Western Europe in ruins.

2. Secretary of State George Marshall argued that the United States had to act quickly. He proposed a bold plan to offer massive economic assistance to help revive Western Europe.

3. QUOTE: "Our policy is directed not against any country or doctrine, but against hunger, poverty, desperation, and chaos."

4. Marshall Plan aid helped spark a dramatic economic recovery. The United States thus achieved its goals of reviving Western Europe and containing Communism.

D. INTERNATIONAL ORGANIZATIONS

1. The United States organized and joined the United Nations to promote international peace and maintain the balance of power.

2. The United States organized and joined the NATO alliance to defend Western Europe from Soviet expansion. NATO represented an example of COLLECTIVE SECURITY, since each member nation pledged military support if any nation in the alliance was attacked. Forming the NATO alliance marked a decisive break from America's prewar policy of isolationism.

E. THE BERLIN BLOCKADE AND AIRLIFT

1. The Soviet Union precipitated the first Cold War test of wills when Stalin unilaterally closed all land routes into West Berlin. His action represented a deliberate attempt to force the United States and its allies to either abandon West Berlin or risk a military confrontation with the Soviet Union. The Berlin Blockade thus represented a major test of Truman's commitment to his administration's policy of containment.

2. Truman surprised Stalin by ordering a massive airlift of supplies into West Berlin. The constant roar of Allied planes over West Berlin provided a vivid demonstration of American power and will. As the Berlin Airlift succeeded, tensions slowly eased and Stalin reopened road and rail traffic into West Berlin.

F. The FALL OF CHINA

1. A long-standing civil war between the Nationalists, led by Chiang Kai-shek, and the Communists, led by Mao Zedong, divided China. Despite massive American aid, Chiang's forces steadily lost ground.

2. On October 1, 1949, Mao triumphantly announced the birth of the People's Republic of China. The United States interpreted the "fall of China" as part of a menacing and unified Communist monolith. Truman therefore refused to recognize Mao's new government in Beijing.

3. Chiang and the remnants of his defeated army fled to Formosa (renamed Taiwan), an island located 100 miles from the Chinese mainland. The United States recognized the government in Taiwan as representing all of China.

4. The "fall of China" contributed to heightened anticommunist hysteria in the United States.

G. THE KOREAN WAR

1. Korea occupies a strategic peninsula that borders China and Russia and extends to within 100 miles of Japan. Both China and Japan view the peninsula as essential to their national security.

2. After World War II, the United States and the Soviet Union agreed to divide Korea at the 38th parallel. The Soviets quickly established a Communist government in North Korea, and the United States supported a non-communist government in South Korea.

3. On June 25, 1950, the North Korean army suddenly invaded South Korea. The surprise attack stunned the United States. Truman viewed the invasion as a test of containment. He also saw it as an opportunity to prove that the Democrats were not "soft" on Communism.

4. Supported by the United States, the United Nations Security Council condemned the North Korean aggression and called upon member nations to aid South Korea. This marked the first collective military action by the United Nations.

5. Within days, American forces commanded by General MacArthur rushed into South Korea. The American forces formed the core of a U.N. army that included units from fourteen other nations. It is important to note that Truman chose to fight the war under the auspices of the U.N. As a result, he did not ask Congress for a declaration of war. It is also important to remember that the Korean War was NOT a guerrilla war.

6. By the end of September 1950, MacArthur's army recaptured all of South Korea. The next month, MacArthur confidently crossed the 38th parallel in a bid to reunite the entire Korean peninsula. China, however, then launched a devastating counterattack that caught MacArthur by surprise and drove the U.N. forces back into South Korea.

7. Truman now decided to give up the attempt to unify Korea. He instead adopted a policy of fighting a limited war to save South Korea. MacArthur publicly questioned Truman's decision, saying, "We must win. There is no substitute for victory." This open act of insubordination forced Truman to remove MacArthur from his command.

8. The Korean War continued for another two years. The North Koreans finally signed an armistice agreement, providing for a cease-fire that left the border between the two Koreas along the 38th parallel. About 30,000 U.S. troops remain stationed in South Korea.

9. The Korean War strengthened American ties with Japan and South Korea, while at the same time exacerbating tensions with China and the Soviet Union. The prolonged stalemate contributed to public frustration that helped elect Eisenhower in 1952.

CHAPTER 28
DOMESTIC DEVELOPMENTS DURING THE TRUMAN YEARS, 1945–1952

A. THE SECOND RED SCARE

1. The Communist victory in China, followed by the outbreak of the Korean War, shocked America. Public apprehension deepened when the Soviet Union exploded an atomic bomb, thus ending America's nuclear monopoly.
2. These stunning reversals heightened the public's fear that Communist agents had infiltrated the State Department and other sensitive government agencies.
3. Concern with internal security became more intense as Cold War tensions increased. The House Un-American Activities Committee (HUAC) soon began a major investigation of Communist subversives within the United States.
4. Prodded by the relentless investigations of Richard Nixon, HUAC discovered that a prominent State Department official named Alger Hiss had been a Soviet spy in the 1930s.
5. The Red Scare even extended to Hollywood. Motion picture executives drew up a "blacklist" of about 500 writers, directors, and actors who were suspended from work for their alleged support of left-wing political beliefs and associations.
6. The popularity of movies about alien invaders from outer space also reflected the anxieties caused by the Red Scare.
7. It is interesting to note that Richard Nixon, John F. Kennedy, and Joseph McCarthy all launched their political careers after World War II as strong anticommunists.

B. McCARTHYISM

1. Joseph McCarthy, a previously obscure senator from Wisconsin, skillfully exploited the political climate of fear engendered by the Red Scare. On February 9, 1950, McCarthy told an audience in Wheeling, West Virginia, that America's foreign policy failures could be traced to Communist infiltration of the State Department.

2. McCarthy's practice of making unsubstantiated accusations of disloyalty without evidence became known as McCARTHYISM. His campaign of innuendo and half-truths made him one of the most feared and powerful politicians in America.

3. QUOTE: "This is the time of the Cold War...The reason why we find ourselves in the position of impotency is not because our only powerful enemy has sent men to invade our shores, but rather because of the traitorous actions of those who have been treated so well by this nation. It has not been the less fortunate or members of minority groups who have been selling this nation out, but rather those who have had all the benefits that the wealthiest nation on earth has had to offer." Senator Joseph McCarthy

4. McCarthy finally caused his own downfall when he launched a televised investigation of the U.S. Army. A national audience of more than 20 million people watched as McCarthy bullied witnesses, twisted people's testimony, and used phony evidence. The Army-McCarthy hearings swiftly turned public sentiment against McCarthy.

C. THE FAIR DEAL

1. Truman's proposed program of social and economic reforms is known as the Fair Deal.

2. The Fair Deal included proposals to raise the minimum wage, expand Social Security benefits, build more public housing, and increase federal aid to education. It did NOT include proposals to nationalize basic American industries.

3. Truman's chances of getting his Fair Deal legislation passed diminished when Republicans took control of both the House and the Senate following the 1946 Congressional elections.

D. THE TAFT-HARTLEY ACT, 1947

1. Passed as part of the Second New Deal, the Wagner Act protected the right of workers to join unions while also banning "unfair practices" previously used by employers against labor unions.
2. Congress passed the Taft-Hartley Act as a response to the growth of union power and an outbreak of labor strikes after World War II.
3. Congress designed the Taft-Hartley Act to curb the power of labor unions. For example, the act made closed shops illegal. In a closed shop, only union members can be hired.
4. The Taft-Hartley Act demonstrated the influence of conservative business leaders, who believed that unions were abusing their power and that widespread strikes endangered America's defense efforts.

E. CIVIL RIGHTS

1. President Truman appointed a commission that issued a report calling for a federal anti-lynching law, a civil rights division within the Justice Department, and a permanent Fair Employment Practices Committee.
2. Segregationist delegates from the Deep South protested Truman's civil rights proposals by walking out of the 1948 Democratic Convention.
3. Led by South Carolina Governor Strom Thurmond, segregationists formed the Dixiecrat Party.
4. Although Congress refused to pass any of his civil rights proposals, President Truman did issue an executive order ending racial segregation in the armed forces.
5. It is important to remember that Truman desegregated the Army before the outbreak of the Korean War. As a result, U.S. forces fought the Korean War in integrated combat units.

CHAPTER 29
THE 1950s

A. THE COLD WAR AND SPUTNIK

1. Both the United States and the Soviet Union had exploded hydrogen bombs by 1954. As a result, a nuclear standoff that Winston Churchill called the "balance of terror" seemed ominously real. Millions of American public school students hid under their desks as part of civil defense "Duck and Cover" drills.

2. President Eisenhower and his Secretary of State John Foster Dulles declared that the United States would no longer become involved in expensive limited conflicts such as the Korean War. Instead, Dulles announced a new strategic policy called MASSIVE RETALIATION. This meant that the United States would consider using its nuclear weapons to halt Communist aggression. To threaten the use of nuclear weapons would require nerves of steel. Journalists soon called Dulles' policy of going to the brink of nuclear war without going over the edge BRINKSMANSHIP.

3. On October 4, 1957, the Soviet Union successfully launched Sputnik, the first space satellite to orbit the Earth. Sputnik jolted Americans' self-confidence. Congress responded by creating the National Aeronautics and Space Administration (NASA) to compete with the Soviet space program. Congress also passed the National Defense Education Act to fund accelerated science and math programs in the nation's public schools.

4. In 1956, President Eisenhower successfully mediated the Suez Crisis.

5. In his Farewell Address, Eisenhower noted that the rise of a "military-industrial complex" had contributed to economic growth. However, he warned that the growing coalition between business and the military had "the potential for the disastrous rise of misplaced power" that could pose a threat to American democracy.

B. UNPRECEDENTED PROSPERITY

1. The 1950s witnessed a period of unprecedented prosperity.
2. Cold War defense spending played a key role in fueling economic growth.

C. SUBURBANIZATION

1. Robust economic growth sparked a strong demand for new homes. William Levitt successfully applied assembly-line production techniques to building homes.
2. The G.I. Bill enabled veterans to buy new homes with little or no down payments.
3. A system of new highways also promoted suburban growth. Supported by President Eisenhower, the Federal Highway Act of 1956 appropriated $25 billion for a ten-year project to construct a 40,000-mile system of interstate highways. These new interstates accelerated suburban growth by enabling people to work in the cities and commute to their homes in the suburbs.

D. THE NEW CULT OF DOMESTICITY

1. By 1960 nearly three-fourths of all American women between the ages of 20 and 24 were married. The soaring marriage and birth rates following World War II encouraged a return to traditional gender roles, in which men were breadwinners and women were housewives.
2. *Life Magazine* devoted a full issue to the role of women. *Life*'s team of writers and photographers glowingly depicted the joys of working with the PTA, cooking meals, and sewing clothes. They did NOT recommend that women complete college before getting married.

E. POPULAR CULTURE

1. By 1957 American families owned over 40 million television sets, or almost as many sets as there were families. Many families organized their daily schedules around such popular shows as *I Love Lucy*, *The Honeymooners*, *Davy Crockett*, *The Mickey Mouse Club*, and *Leave It to Beaver*.
2. Television, the beginning of rock and roll, Levittown housing, and beatniks were all important cultural developments during the 1950s.
3. James Dean and Marlon Brando were popular actors who embodied youthful rebellion.
4. Dr. Jonas Salk developed a vaccine to prevent polio.

F. SOCIAL CRITICS

1. Critics complained about the mindless conformity and excessive materialism that seemed so prevalent in American suburbs. It is interesting to note that they did NOT criticize the suburbs for political corruption.
2. David Riesman (*The Lonely Crowd*) and William H. Whyte (*The Organization Man*) studied alienation in large corporations.
3. Sloan Wilson's novel *The Man in the Gray Flannel Suit* criticized middle-class conformity, or what Wilson called "a frantic parade to nowhere."

G. THE BEAT GENERATION

1. A small but culturally influential group of self-described "beats" also rejected suburban America's carefree consumption and mindless conformity.
2. Jack Kerouac was the best known Beat Generation author. His autobiographical novel *On the Road* reflected the alienation of the Beat Generation.

H. ARTISTIC REBELS

1. Edward Hopper's paintings captured the loneliness and alienation of American life. For an excellent example, see *Office in a Small City*.
2. Jackson Pollock refused to portray specific subject matter. Instead, he created Abstract Expressionist paintings by spontaneously dripping oil on a canvas spread across the floor. For an excellent example, see *Autumn Rhythm*.

CHAPTER 30
THE CIVIL RIGHTS MOVEMENT, 1954–1960

A. THE DOUBLE V CAMPAIGN

1. During World War II, African Americans fought in segregated units led by white officers. The soldiers were painfully aware of the contradiction between fighting for the freedom of others while enduring racial injustice themselves.

2. The Double V Campaign called for African Americans to fight for victory over fascism in Europe and then fight for victory over racism at home.

B. *BROWN V. BOARD OF EDUCATION*, 1954

1. Since its founding in 1909, the National Association for the Advancement of Colored People (NAACP) had adopted the strategy of filing legal cases to win civil rights for African Americans.

2. When the 1953–54 school year opened, 2.5 million African American children attended all-black schools in 17 southern states and the District of Columbia. Led by Thurgood Marshall, the NAACP legal team chose to challenge state laws mandating segregation in their public schools.

3. Thurgood Marshall argued that segregated schools in Topeka, Kansas, were unconstitutional because they denied African American children the "equal protection of the law" guaranteed by the Fourteenth Amendment.

4. Led by Chief Justice Earl Warren, the Supreme Court agreed with Thurgood Marshall. In a unanimous decision, the Court overturned the long-standing "separate but equal" doctrine established in *Plessy v. Ferguson*.

5. QUOTE: "Does segregation of children in public schools solely on the basis of race, even though the physical facilities and other tangible factors may be equal, deprive children of the minority group of equal educational opportunities? We believe that it does...We conclude that in the field of public education, the doctrine of separate but equal has no place. Separate educational facilities are inherently unequal. Therefore, we hold that the plaintiffs and others similarly situated for whom the actions have been brought are, by reason of the segregation complained of, deprived of the equal protection of the laws guaranteed by the Fourteenth Amendment." Earl Warren

C. PRESIDENT EISENHOWER AND LITTLE ROCK, 1957

1. Although President Eisenhower accepted the *Brown* decision, he thought that it was a mistake. Ike did not use his enormous personal prestige to provide moral support for the civil rights movement. He privately believed that "You cannot change people's hearts merely by laws."

2. A crisis in Little Rock, Arkansas, forced Eisenhower to act. The city school board adopted a desegregation plan that called for nine black students to attend Little Rock's Central High School. The crisis began when an angry white mob surrounded the school and threatened to attack the nine black children.

3. This blatant display of resistance forced President Eisenhower to act. The President felt that he had a constitutional obligation to enforce the Brown decision. He therefore ordered 1,100 paratroopers to Little Rock to protect the black students and enforce the Supreme Court's desegregation order. Eisenhower thus became the first president since Reconstruction to use federal troops to enforce the rights of African Americans.

4. QUOTE: "The very basis of our individual rights and freedoms rests upon the certainty that the President and the Executive Branch of government will support and insure the carrying out of the decisions of the federal courts, even, when necessary, with all the means at the President's command."

D. THE MONTGOMERY BUS BOYCOTT, 1955-1956

1. On December 1, 1955, a white Montgomery City Lines bus driver ordered a 42-year-old black seamstress named Rosa Parks to give up her seat to a white passenger. Parks refused by saying just one word, "No."

2. Rosa Parks' refusal to give up her seat sparked the Montgomery Bus Boycott. Led by her young minister, the 26-year-old Dr. Martin Luther King, Jr., the black community supported Parks by boycotting Montgomery's bus system. The boycott finally ended 15 months later, when the Supreme Court ruled that segregation on public buses was unconstitutional.

E. DR. KING AND NONVIOLENT CIVIL DISOBEDIENCE

1. The Montgomery Bus Boycott catapulted Dr. King to national prominence. He soon emerged as America's foremost civil rights leader.

2. Dr. King inspired his followers with a message of nonviolent civil disobedience derived from the writings of Henry David Thoreau and the actions of Mahatma Gandhi in India.

3. QUOTE: "During the days of the Montgomery Bus Boycott, I came to see the power of nonviolence more and more. As I lived through the actual experience of protest, nonviolence became more than a useful method, it became a way of life." Dr. Martin Luther King, Jr.

4. Following the success of the Montgomery Bus Boycott, King founded the Southern Christian Leadership Conference (SCLC) to apply the principles of nonviolent civil disobedience throughout the South.

F. THE SIT-IN MOVEMENT

1. Despite the victories in Little Rock and Montgomery, segregation remained entrenched throughout the South. For example, lunch counters still remained segregated.

2. Dr. King's philosophy of nonviolent civil disobedience inspired four black college students in Greensboro, North Carolina, to take action. Calling segregation "evil pure and simple," the Greensboro Four sat down at a "whites only" Woolworth lunch counter and ordered coffee and apple pie. When the waitress refused to take their order, the students remained seated. Their "sit-in" tactic worked. Six months later, the Greensboro Woolworth desegregated its lunch counters.

3. The Greensboro sit-ins energized student-led protests across the South. A growing wave of student protesters held "read-ins" at libraries, "watch-ins" at movie theaters, and "wade-ins" at beaches.

4. Encouraged by Ella Baker, black and white students formed the Student Nonviolent Coordinating Committee (SNCC) to facilitate student activism.

CHAPTER 31
THE TUMULTUOUS SIXTIES—PART I

A. THE 1960 PRESIDENTIAL ELECTION

1. The Republicans nominated Vice President Richard Nixon. The veteran politician promised to continue Ike's popular policies.

2. The Democrats countered by nominating Senator John F. Kennedy of Massachusetts. Kennedy was young, handsome, and a Roman Catholic. Many worried that voters would reject Kennedy because of his religion.

3. Kennedy forcefully dealt with the religion issue in a speech to a group of Protestant ministers in Houston. He firmly rejected the belief that a Catholic president would have divided loyalties between America and Rome. "I am not the Catholic candidate for President," Kennedy reminded his audience. "I am the Democratic Party's candidate for President who happens also to be a Catholic."

4. The 1960 presidential election included a series of televised debates between Kennedy and Nixon. Kennedy dispelled doubts about his age and inexperience. While Nixon appeared tense and tired, Kennedy radiated confidence and poise. He impressed viewers with his crisp, fact-filled answers and inspiring pledge to lead America into a "New Frontier."

B. THE NEW FRONTIER

1. The vigorous young President and his glamorous wife fascinated the American public. The First Family's youthful charm seemed like a fairy tale come to life. A popular musical at that time portrayed the romance and adventure of King Arthur's court at Camelot. Kennedy and his dedicated band of advisors reminded many of a modern-day Camelot.

2. The Peace Corps was JFK's most popular New Frontier program. Thousands of idealistic young Americans volunteered to help battle hunger, disease, and illiteracy in Third World countries.

C. THE BAY OF PIGS INVASION

1. Thousands of Cubans fled to the United States following Castro's rise to power and growing alliance with the Soviet Union. Shortly after he became President, Kennedy learned that the CIA had been secretly training a small army of about 1,200 Cuban exiles. The plan called for them to invade Cuba at the Bay of Pigs on the island's southern coast. The armed exile army would then ignite a popular uprising that would lead to the overthrow of Castro and his Communist government.

2. The invasion turned into a disastrous failure. A Cuban army of 20,000 men, supported by tanks, attacked and surrounded the exiles. Despite their heroic resistance, the outnumbered exiles were forced to surrender.

3. The Bay of Pigs fiasco handed Kennedy an embarrassing defeat that damaged his international credibility.

D. THE CUBAN MISSILE CRISIS

1. The Bay of Pigs invasion alarmed Soviet Premier Nikita Khrushchev. In a daring gamble to protect the Castro regime, Khrushchev secretly allowed Soviet technicians to install nuclear-armed missiles inside Cuba. It is important to note that the Organization of American States did NOT invite the Soviets to put missiles in Cuba.

2. High-flying U-2 spy planes discovered the missile sites. After careful deliberation, Kennedy announced a "quarantine," or blockade, of Cuba to prevent the Soviets from sending more missiles to Cuba.

3. Following tense negotiations, Khrushchev agreed to withdraw his missiles in exchange for an American pledge not to invade Cuba and overthrow Castro.

E. THE CIVIL RIGHTS MOVEMENT, 1961–1965

1. The sit-in movement proved that nonviolent direct action protests would work. Within a short time, a growing number of blacks and whites joined Dr. King's "coalition of conscience" to protest segregation.

2. In May 1961, the Congress of Racial Equality (CORE) sent an integrated group of 13 "freedom riders" on a bus trip that began in Washington, D.C., and was scheduled to end in New Orleans. Their goal was to find out if Southern cities were obeying a 1960 Supreme Court decision banning segregation in bus stations. They quickly learned that the Court's order was being ignored. Klansmen in Alabama attacked the Freedom Riders and bombed their bus. Aroused by these acts of violence, Attorney General Robert Kennedy convinced the Interstate Commerce Commission to issue an order banning segregation in interstate bus terminals.

3. The focus of the civil rights struggle now shifted to Birmingham, Alabama. The city Commissioner of Public Safety, Eugene "Bull" Conner, promptly arrested over 3,000 demonstrators, including Dr. King. While in jail, Dr. King wrote his famous "Letter from Birmingham City Jail," in which he defended civil disobedience as a justified response to unjust segregation laws.

4. The violence in Birmingham outraged President Kennedy. He called upon Congress to pass a sweeping civil rights bill that would prohibit segregation in public places, speed up school integration, and ban discrimination in hiring practices.

5. Dr. King and other black leaders called for a massive March on Washington to demonstrate public support for the bill. As millions of Americans watched on television, over 250,000 black and white marchers staged the largest civil rights demonstration in American history. The climax of the day occurred when Dr. King delivered his famous "I Have a Dream" speech. The March on Washington marked a historic moment, when the civil rights movement achieved its greatest unity.

6. Following the assassination of President Kennedy, President Johnson made passing the civil rights bill his top priority. LBJ proudly signed the 1964 Civil Rights Act into law on July 2, 1964. The new law barred discrimination in public facilities such as hotels, restaurants, and theaters. The act also outlawed discrimination in employment on the basis of race, creed, national origin, or sex. It is important to note that women's groups would use the clause barring discrimination based on sex to secure government support for greater equality in education and employment.

7. Civil rights leaders now turned to the issue of voting rights. In 1964, civil rights organizations mounted a major campaign to register black voters in Mississippi. Known as the Mississippi Freedom Summer, the effort attracted several hundred idealistic black and white college students from across the country. However, the volunteers could not overcome the determined opposition of segregationists, who used poll taxes, literacy tests, and violence to intimidate black voters.

8. The Mississippi Freedom Summer demonstrated the need for strong federal action to overcome long-established obstacles designed to prevent blacks from voting. The Voting Rights Act of 1965 outlawed literacy tests and other devices that prevented African Americans from voting. At the same time, the Twenty-Fourth Amendment outlawed the poll tax in federal elections.

F. LBJ AND THE GREAT SOCIETY

1. President Johnson offered his vision of a new American society in a commencement address delivered at the University of Michigan. "The Great Society," Johnson explained, "rests on abundance and liberty for all. It demands an end to poverty and racial injustice." Johnson pledged to rebuild decaying cities, renew American education, and restore the natural environment.

2. Spurred by Johnson's unique mix of cajoling and coercion, Congress passed a series of Great Society programs that included providing Medicare and Medicaid for the elderly, declaring war on poverty, revitalizing decaying inner cities, funding job training, and creating Head Start programs for disadvantaged children. It is important to note that Head Start and other Great Society preschool programs were NOT an extension of New Deal policies.

3. The Great Society did NOT guarantee full employment, establish the Peace Corps, or create Social Security.

4. The Immigration Act of 1965 ended the system of national origins quotas created during the 1920s. It is important to note that this led to a significant increase in immigration from Latin America and Asia.

G. THE GREAT SOCIETY AND THE NEW DEAL

1. Both the Great Society and the New Deal demonstrated a willingness to use the power of the federal government to address social problems.

2. Both the Great Society and the New Deal included programs to promote the arts, help the elderly, encourage the construction of housing, and raise employment levels.

3. The New Deal did NOT include programs specifically intended to promote civil rights. In contrast, the Great Society included landmark bills to promote African American civil and voting rights.

H. THE WARREN COURT AND THE RIGHTS REVOLUTION

1. The Warren Court issued a number of landmark decisions that promoted what historians call the "Rights Revolution."

2. In *Miranda v. Arizona*, the Court ruled that police have a duty to inform arrested persons of their rights, including the right to remain silent.

3. In *Baker v. Carr*, the Court established the principle of "one man, one vote," by requiring some state legislatures to reapportion their congressional districts.

CHAPTER 32
THE TUMULTUOUS SIXTIES—PART II

A. THE VIETNAM WAR: INVOLVEMENT AND ESCALATION

1. Following World War II, the French became entangled in a costly guerilla war with Vietnamese forces led by Ho Chi Minh. It is important to remember that Ho Chi Minh was both a Vietnamese nationalist leader and a dedicated Communist.
2. The French withdrew from Vietnam after suffering a disastrous defeat at the Battle of Dien Bien Phu. The United States then replaced France as the leading Western power in Indochina.
3. Both President Eisenhower and President Kennedy used the DOMINO THEORY to justify their decision to send military advisors to help South Vietnam resist Communist subversion from North Vietnam. According to the DOMINO THEORY, the fall of South Vietnam would inevitably lead to the spread of Communism to Laos, Cambodia, and other nearby countries.
4. QUOTE: "If Indo-China were to fall and if its fall led to the loss of all of Southeast Asia, then the United States might eventually be forced back to Hawaii, as it was before the Second World War." Secretary of State Dean Rusk
5. President Johnson inherited an increasingly dangerous situation in South Vietnam. On August 4, 1964, he received unsubstantiated reports that North Vietnamese gunboats had fired on two American destroyers patrolling in the Gulf of Tonkin. The next day, Johnson asked Congress to pass a resolution authorizing him to take "all necessary measures to repel any armed attack against the forces of the United States and to prevent further aggression." The Gulf of Tonkin Resolution thus marked an important turning point in the

Vietnam War by giving President Johnson a blank check to escalate American involvement.

6. The situation in South Vietnam continued to worsen. In March 1965, LBJ took the fateful step of ordering a massive escalation of American forces in Vietnam. By 1967, almost 500,000 American soldiers guarded South Vietnam's cities and patrolled its rice paddies.

B. THE VIETNAM WAR: HAWKS VERSUS DOVES

1. When President Johnson escalated the Vietnam War, about two-thirds of the American public approved his decision. Known as HAWKS, supporters of the war argued that the United States was fighting a just cause to defend the freedom of South Vietnam.

2. As costs and casualties steadily mounted, a growing number of people began to question America's involvement in Vietnam. Known as DOVES, opponents of the war argued that America could not win a guerrilla war in Asia. Instead of saving South Vietnam, American bombs were destroying it.

3. Senator William Fulbright criticized American involvement as an example of what he called "the arrogance of power."

4. Hippies believed that love and not war was the solution to America's problems. They argued that peace could replace war by creating a new way of life they called the COUNTERCULTURE. Hippies often congregated in huge outdoor music concerts such as the Woodstock Music Festival.

5. President Johnson attempted to reassure the American people by promising, "victory was just around the corner." However, the Viet Cong and North Vietnamese forces undermined LBJ's prediction by launching an all-out attack called the Tet Offensive.

6. The Tet Offensive marked a key turning point in the Vietnam War. Although American forces regained the initiative and won a military victory, the Tet Offensive triggered widespread domestic dissent in the United States. As more and more Americans questioned LBJ's handling of the war, his credibility plummeted. On March 31, 1968, Johnson told a stunned national television audience that he would not seek another term as president.

C. BLACK POWER

1. By the mid-1960s, many civil rights activists began to recognize that while Supreme Court decisions and new laws could address legal forms of discrimination, they could not solve the pressing economic problems of blacks living in urban ghettos. As more and more African Americans became frustrated with the slow pace of reform, they turned to a new group of leaders who championed a more militant call to action than the nonviolent approach advocated by Dr. King.

2. Malcolm X was a charismatic Black Muslim leader who preached a philosophy of militant black separatism.

3. QUOTE: "When I say fight for independence right here, I don't mean any nonviolent fight, or turn-the-other-cheek fight. Those days are gone, those days are over." Malcolm X

4. Following the assassination of Malcolm X in 1965, Stokely Carmichael emerged as America's most widely recognized militant black leader. Carmichael excited his followers by boldly calling for "black power." As explained by Carmichael, BLACK POWER meant that blacks should build economic and political power by building black-owned businesses and electing black public officials. It is important to note that BLACK POWER also emphasized black pride by encouraging African Americans to wear African clothing and celebrate black history.

5. A combination of the assassination of Malcolm X, urban riots, SNCC's shift to the principles of BLACK POWER, and the rise of the Black Panthers in California all contributed to the increased radicalization of many African American in the late 1960s.

D. BETTY FRIEDAN AND THE WOMEN'S MOVEMENT

1. Women played an active role in the Civil Rights Movement. This experience sharpened their awareness that women also suffered from unfair discrimination.

2. Betty Friedan was the first to express the sense of injustice felt by many women. Her book, *The Feminine Mystique*, challenged the cult of domesticity that had prevailed since the end of World War II.

3. In 1966, Friedan and other women activists formed the National Organization for Women (NOW) to work for equal rights and to challenge sex discrimination in the workplace.

E. RACHEL CARSON AND THE ENVIRONMENTAL MOVEMENT

1. Rachel Carson was an American marine biologist whose groundbreaking book, *Silent Spring*, warned that the unrestricted use of DDT and other chemical pesticides posed a dangerous threat to both human and animal life. Carson called for a ban on DDT and other chemical pesticides.

2. QUOTE: "The history of life on Earth has been a history of interaction between living things and their surroundings. To a large extent, the physical form and habits of the Earth's vegetation and its animal life have been molded by the environment ... The most alarming of all man's assaults upon the environment is the contamination of air, earth, rivers, and sea with dangerous and even lethal materials." Rachel Carson

3. *Silent Spring* helped launch the national environmental movement. Beginning in 1970, millions of Americans participated in Earth Day activities to help clean up the environment.

4. The environmental movement also expressed concerns about the waste produced by nuclear power plants. An accident at the Three Mile Island nuclear power plant intensified these concerns.

F. RALPH NADER AND THE CONSUMER MOVEMENT

1. Ralph Nader rose to prominence as the author of *Unsafe at Any Speed*, a scathing critique of the safety record of American automobile companies.

2. Nader's writings helped spark a reform movement for consumer rights.

G. ANDY WARHOL AND POP ART

1. Andy Warhol was an American artist who was a leading figure in the artistic style known as Pop Art.

2. Warhol's series of paintings of Campbell's soup cans provide a particularly well-known example of Pop Art.

CHAPTER 33
THE 1970s—NIXON, CARTER, AND THE AGE OF LIMITS

A. NIXON AND VIETNAM

1. Nixon inherited a difficult situation in Vietnam. At the time of his inauguration in 1969, 540,000 American soldiers were still in Vietnam. A growing number of Americans wanted to end a war that had already claimed the lives of 31,000 U.S. soldiers.

2. Nixon chose to follow a policy of gradually withdrawing American forces while simultaneously replacing them with South Vietnamese soldiers. Nixon believed that his policy of VIETNAMIZATION would bring "peace with honor."

3. Nixon appealed to "the great silent majority" of Americans to support Vietnamization. According to Nixon, the SILENT MAJORITY included hard-working "nonshouters and nondemonstrators" who "care about a strong United States, about patriotism, about moral and spiritual values." This conservative group lived in fast-growing states in the South and West, where they formed the core of a new Republican coalition of voters.

4. Nixon's strategy of Vietnamization appeared to be working. Then on April 30, 1970, he surprised the nation by announcing that he had ordered American troops into Cambodia to disrupt North Vietnamese supply lines. Outraged college students protested the Cambodian invasion on campuses across America. Tragedy struck at Kent State University in Ohio, when nervous National Guard soldiers opened fire on demonstrating students, killing four and wounding nine.

5. The shootings at Kent State triggered a tidal wave of student protests. However, despite the student outcry, the Silent Majority continued to support Nixon.

6. After nearly three years of continued fighting, Nixon announced that the U.S. and North Vietnamese negotiators had reached an agreement known as the Paris Accords that would "end the war and bring peace with honor to Vietnam and Southeast Asia."

7. The North Vietnamese ignored their promise "to maintain the cease fire." Just two years after signing the Paris Accords, they launched a massive invasion that forced the South Vietnamese government to surrender on April 30, 1975.

B. THE LEGACY OF VIETNAM

1. Congress responded to the abuse of the president's war-making power by repealing the Gulf of Tonkin Resolution and passing the War Powers Act. The new law restricted the president's ability to unilaterally deploy troops into war zones without congressional approval.

2. Many Americans questioned foreign entanglements that might become "another Vietnam." This skepticism about military interventions became known as the "Vietnam Syndrome."

C. NIXON AND DÉTENTE

1. As the leader of the free world, the United States attempted to contain Soviet expansion and isolate the People's Republic of China. Nixon believed that the time had come to pursue bold policy initiatives that would reshape global politics.

2. In February 1972, Nixon became the first American president to visit the People's Republic of China. His historic visit opened a new era of cultural exchanges and trade between the two countries. The United States and the People's Republic of China established formal diplomatic relations in 1979, during the Carter administration.

3. Three months after returning from China, Nixon once again stunned the world by becoming the first American president to visit Moscow. During the seven-day summit, Nixon and Soviet Premier Leonid Brezhnev signed a Strategic Arms Limitation Treaty (SALT I) that placed limits on both the number of intercontinental ballistic missiles and the construction of anti-ballistic missile systems.

4. The SALT I treaty signaled the beginning of a new period of relaxed tensions between the two Cold War rivals that is known as DÉTENTE.

D. THE ARAB OIL EMBARGO

1. In October 1973, Egypt and Syria attacked Israel on Yom Kippur, the holiest day of the Jewish year. Although American military aid enabled Israel to prevail, the effects of the Yom Kippur War continued.

2. Nixon's decision to help Israel angered many oil-rich Arab nations. As the most important members of the Organization of Petroleum Exporting Countries (OPEC), they had the power to reduce the supply of oil and raise prices. On October 20, 1973, they chose to do both.

3. The Arab oil embargo quickly disrupted daily life in the United States. Motorists who had assumed that gasoline would always be cheap and plentiful found themselves waiting in lines up to two miles long to buy fuel that had nearly doubled in price.

4. The effects of the energy crisis did not end with the lifting of the embargo in April 1974. The oil embargo marked the end of the post-World War II economic boom and the beginning of an inflationary spiral that plagued the U.S. economy during the rest of the 1970s. It is interesting to note that the Arab oil embargo did NOT prompt Congress to pass anti-pollution legislation.

E. THE WATERGATE SCANDAL AND THE FALL OF NIXON

1. On June 17, 1972, police arrested five burglars who had broken into the headquarters of the Democratic National Committee at the Watergate apartment and office complex in Washington, D.C.

2. President Nixon was never directly implicated in the Watergate break-in. However, instead of firing the corrupt officials responsible for the crime, he chose to "play it tough" and attempt to cover-up the scandal. Two months after the break-in, President Nixon announced that a "complete investigation" revealed "no one in the White House staff, no one in this administration, presently employed, was involved

in this very bizarre incident." Nixon was lying. Evidence later revealed that the break-in was part of a much larger campaign of "dirty tricks" financed by the Committee to Reelect the President.

3. The House Judiciary Committee ultimately voted to recommend that Nixon be impeached for obstruction of justice. This action provides a particularly vivid example of the constitutional process of checks and balances.

4. On August 9, 1974, Richard Nixon became the first president to resign from office. Vice President Gerald Ford then became the nation's 38th president. "My fellow Americans," Ford declared, "our long national nightmare is over."

F. THE FORD ADMINISTRATION, 1974-1977

1. A month after Nixon's resignation, Ford surprised the nation by granting the former president a full pardon. Ford's popularity plummeted, as almost two-thirds of the American people disagreed with his decision.

2. Although unpopular, the pardon did help put aside the Watergate issue. Polls emphatically showed that the public ranked inflation as the nation's most pressing domestic problem.

3. Prices rose by over 20 percent between 1974 and 1976. The soaring price of energy, along with the rising cost of health care, a growing national debt, and the high cost of the Vietnam War, all contributed to inflationary pressures. Although the savings and loan crisis was a major problem, it did NOT play a major role in causing inflation.

4. Soaring inflation and rising unemployment damaged Ford's popularity. His inability to revive the economy enabled the Democratic candidate Jimmy Carter to win the 1976 presidential election.

G. THE CARTER ADMINISTRATION, 1977-1981

1. Carter began his presidency with high hopes. However, he soon faced a seemingly intractable economic problem. The American economy was simultaneously experiencing a combination of rising unemployment and double-digit inflation. Economists called this unusual phenomenon STAGFLATION.

2. President Carter pursued an idealistic foreign policy. He promised to defend human rights, pledging that his actions would be guided by "fairness, not force."

3. Carter's commitment to patient negotiating achieved a dramatic breakthrough in Middle East diplomacy. In September 1978, he invited Egyptian President Anwar Sadat and Israeli Prime Minister Manachem Begin to meet with him at Camp David, the presidential retreat in Maryland. After 13 days of often tense negotiations, a beaming Carter announced that the two sides had reached an historic peace agreement. The Camp David Accords ended 30 years of intermittent war and hostility between Egypt and Israel.

4. The Camp David Accords marked Carter's greatest triumph. But just over a year later, an Iranian mob stormed the U.S. embassy in Tehran and took over 50 Americans hostage. The hostage crisis plunged the Carter presidency into a diplomatic dilemma it was unable to successfully resolve.

H. THE PRESIDENTIAL ELECTION OF 1980

1. The Iranian hostage crisis, double-digit inflation, and a continued rise in energy prices seriously weakened Carter's popularity.

2. During the campaign, the Republican candidate Ronald Reagan repeatedly asked the American people to answer one question: "Are you better off now than you were four years ago?" On Election Day the voters overwhelmingly answered "no." Reagan and his running mate, George H. W. Bush, won a landslide victory.

I. LANDMARK SUPREME COURT CASES

1. *Roe v. Wade*, 1973—The Court upheld abortion rights for women. The justices based their decision on the right to privacy established in *Griswold v. Connecticut*.

2. *Regents of the University of California v. Bakke*, 1978—The Court struck down the system of rigid affirmative action quotas used at the University of California at Davis Medical School to correct racial injustices in the past. However, the Court also ruled that race could be used as a factor in admission decisions.

CHAPTER 34
KEY EVENTS AND TRENDS, 1980–PRESENT

A. THE NEW CONSERVATIVE COALITION

1. Barry Goldwater was a conservative senator from Arizona who ran for President in 1964. Goldwater and his supporters opposed Great Society programs while favoring a limited federal government, long advocated by states' rights proponents. Although Goldwater lost the election, his conservative influence laid the political foundation for Reagan's rise to power.

2. The growing conservative coalition also included politically active religious conservatives. Founded and led by Jerry Falwell, the Moral Majority argued that feminism, abortion, and other permissive practices were eroding core American "family values."

3. The election of Ronald Reagan in 1980 signaled the rise to power of a new conservative coalition in American politics. Known as the "NEW RIGHT," this conservative coalition included middle-class suburbanites, blue-collar Catholics, evangelical Protestants, and white families living in the Sunbelt.

B. REAGANOMICS

1. Reagan opposed the use of New Deal-type programs to fight stagflation. "Government is not the solution to our problem," Reagan declared. "Government is the problem."

2. Reagan boldly called upon Congress to sharply reduce government funding for social and welfare programs. He argued that these cuts would help curb federal spending and fight inflation. He also asked Congress to enact a three-year, 30-percent cut in personal income taxes. Reagan believed that these cuts would stimulate the economy. And finally, Reagan called upon Congress to reduce government regulation of business. He believed that free-market capitalism would create jobs and promote growth.

3. Reporters promptly labeled the President's supply-side economic program REAGANOMICS. Critics argued that Reaganomics would disproportionally benefit wealthy Americans while hurting the poor and needy.

4. Despite a difficult beginning, Reagan's confidence proved to be justified. America enjoyed a sustained period of economic growth from late 1982 to 1988.

C. U.S.-SOVIET RELATIONS

1. While economic problems received Reagan's highest priority, relations with the Soviet Union dominated his foreign policy. In a speech given on March 8, 1983, Reagan charged the Soviet Union with being "the focus of evil in the modern world." Reagan's "Evil Empire" speech inspired dissidents behind the Iron Curtain.

2. The REAGAN DOCTRINE is the name given to Reagan's strategy to confront and oppose the global influence of the Soviet Union while also supporting anti-Communist forces.

3. The Reagan Doctrine led to a massive American military buildup. In 1983, Reagan proposed a Strategic Defense Initiative as an additional check on Soviet nuclear capability. Reagan envisioned creating a space-based missile defense system capable of striking Soviet missiles before they could reach the United States. The press quickly called Reagan's plan "Star Wars." Meanwhile, critics charged that the expensive program was really directed at cutting funds for domestic programs.

4. Reagan's confrontational approach to the Soviet Union began to change when Mikhail Gorbachev assumed power in 1985. The new Soviet leader initiated an ambitious set of reforms aimed at opening the Soviet system and restructuring its economy.

5. Although Gorbachev and Reagan remained ideological adversaries, they nonetheless agreed to a series of arms reduction measures. As tensions between the two superpowers eased, Gorbachev began to relax the Soviet grip on Eastern Europe.

D. THE G. H. W. BUSH PRESIDENCY, 1989-1993

1. The George H. W. Bush presidency witnessed both the fall of the Berlin Wall (1989) and the collapse of the Soviet Union (1991).
2. On August 2, 1990, Saddam Hussein ordered Iraqi forces to invade Kuwait. President Bush argued that Iraq had to be confronted. The United States could not allow any nation to dominate the Persian Gulf and thus control a major portion of the world's oil supply.
3. Bush skillfully forged an international coalition of 28 nations to force Hussein to withdraw from Kuwait. Led by the United States, Operation Desert Storm successfully crushed Hussein's army and liberated Kuwait.
4. The overwhelming success of Operation Desert Storm led Bush to believe that the Persian Gulf War had ended America's Vietnam Syndrome.

E. THE CLINTON PRESIDENCY, 1993-2001

1. The North American Free Trade Agreement (NAFTA) created a free-trade zone with Canada and Mexico.
2. The World Trade Organization (WTO) was established in 1994 to oversee trade agreements and enforce trade rules.
3. Republican Speaker of the House Newt Gingrich often blocked Clinton's legislative program.
4. The House of Representatives impeached President Clinton for perjury and obstruction of justice. However, the Senate did not uphold these charges.
5. It is important to note that Presidents Andrew Johnson and Bill Clinton were both impeached by the House but not convicted by the Senate.

F. THE G. W. BUSH PRESIDENCY, 2001-2009

1. President George W. Bush ordered American forces to bomb Taliban bases in Afghanistan in the months immediately following the 9/11 attacks of 2001.
2. The United States invasion of Iraq occurred in 2003.

G. KEY DEMOGRAPHIC CHANGES

1. The BABY BOOM generation includes 76 million people born between 1946 and 1964. As the Baby Boomers begin to retire, they will put increasing financial pressure on the Social Security system.
2. The SUNBELT includes a region that stretches from the Carolinas to Southern California. By 2000, a majority of Americans lived in the Sunbelt states.
3. The Immigration Act of 1965 triggered a major new wave of immigration to America. Between 1990 and 2000, over 10 million people immigrants entered the United States. The largest number came from Latin America and Asia.

H. WOMEN'S RIGHTS

1. The Equal Rights Amendment was NOT ratified. Activists led by Phyllis Schlafly successfully opposed the amendment, arguing that it would take away legal rights from wives and negatively influence family life.
2. Geraldine Ferraro was the first female vice-presidential candidate. She ran on the 1984 Democratic ticket with Walter Mondale. Ferraro and Mondale ran a spirited campaign but were defeated by the Republican ticket of Reagan and Bush.
3. During the 1980s a higher proportion of women were in the labor force than at any previous time in the 20th century.
4. During the 1980s and '90s, feminists achieved significant increases in the number of women entering professional jobs. However, women continued to earn less than men.
5. During the 1980s and '90s, feminists continued to challenge traditional views of women's roles.

PART 2
SUPER FAST REVIEW

CHAPTER 1: PRE-COLUMBIAN AMERICA

1. PREHISTORIC HUNTERS—reached America by crossing a land bridge connecting Siberia with Alaska.
2. PRE-COLUMBIAN PEOPLES—did NOT develop wheeled vehicles, water wheels, or have tribal property rights.
3. PACIFIC NORTHWEST—tribes relied on hunting and fishing.
4. ANASAZIS—a sedentary agricultural people living in the Southwest.
5. IROQUOIS—lived in permanent settlements and formed an important political alliance.
6. CREEKS, CHEROKEE, AND CHICKASAW—all lived in the Eastern Woodlands.
7. SIOUX—nomadic tribes
8. MATRILINEAL—Eastern Woodland tribes lived in matrilineal societies, in which inheritance is passed down through the mother; women were the primary farmers among the Eastern Woodland tribes.
9. MAIZE—domesticated before the arrival of the European colonists; would later be exported to Europe.

CHAPTER 2: NEW SPAIN AND NEW FRANCE

1. PORTUGAL—first European nation to conduct regular maritime expeditions in the South Atlantic.
2. SMALLPOX—decimated the Native American population.
3. COLUMBIAN EXCHANGE—exchange of plants, animals, and diseases between Europe and the New World.
4. SPANISH—did NOT recruit bureaucrats from Native Americans; were not motivated by a desire to find a place to trade manufactured goods; had the most contact with the Hopi and Zuni; exploited silver mines in Peru.
5. FLORIDA—discovered and first colonized by Spain.
6. ST. AUGUSTINE—first permanent settlement in the U.S.
7. PUEBLO REVOLT—temporarily drove the Spanish out of New Mexico.
8. NEW FRANCE—based on fur trade and cooperative relations with Native Americans; but very small population and few settlers.
9. EUROPEAN DISEASES—caused a drastic decline in Native American population.

(Side margin text:) SUPER FAST REVIEW

CHAPTER 3: VIRGINA AND THE SOUTHERN COLONIES

1. JOINT-STOCK COMPANY—investors share the risks and profits in proportion to their portion of the total investment.
2. VIRGINIA—founded by a joint-stock company to make a profit; not founded to promote religious toleration.
3. TOBACCO—saved the Virginia colony from economic collapse.
4. MARYLAND—founded as a religious refuge for Roman Catholics.
5. INDENTURED SERVANTS—played a key role in the growth of the early plantation system.
6. BACON'S REBELLION—exposed tensions between the planters and former indentured servants; encouraged planters to import slaves; reduced the power of Native American tribes in Virginia.
7. RICE—most important cash crop in 18th-century South Carolina.
8. INDIGO—required less labor to cultivate than either tobacco or rice.
9. GEORGIA—founded as a buffer between Spanish Florida and South Carolina.
10. COLONIAL CHARTERS—granted as privileges but then considered rights of Englishmen.
11. HOUSE OF BURGESSES—first representative body in the colonies.

CHAPTER 4: THE PURITANS AND THE QUAKERS

1. MAYFLOWER COMPACT—agreement to make political decisions based upon the will of the people.
2. "CITY UPON A HILL"—John Winthrop's sermon expressing the Puritan goal of creating a model Christian community.
3. PURITANS—migrated in family groups; lived in compact communities; valued education; did NOT believe in the innate goodness of human nature; did NOT cultivate cash crops; did NOT allow women to take a leadership role in public affairs.
4. ANNE HUTCHINSON—banished for challenging orthodox Puritan beliefs.
5. ROGER WILLIAMS—banished for advocating separation of church and state and religious toleration.
6. HALFWAY COVENANT—relaxed requirements for church membership; caused by a decline in church membership and religious zeal.
7. NEW ENGLAND CONFEDERATION—early attempt at colonial unity.

8. DOMINION OF NEW ENGLAND—collapsed after the Glorious Revolution.
9. QUAKERS—pacifists, opposed slavery, allowed women to speak publicly; did NOT practice clerical celibacy.
10. PENNSYLVANIA—founded as a refuge for Quakers; diverse mix of ethnic groups; no established church; good relations with Indians; attracted a diverse group of immigrants from Germany, including Dunkers, Moravian Brethren, Mennonites, and Schwenkfelders.
11. LIFE EXPECTANCY—was greater in the New England colonies than in the Chesapeake colonies.
12. KING PHILIP'S WAR—bitter conflict between Native Americans and Massachusetts colonists; led to a drastic decline in the power of Native Americans in the region.

CHAPTER 5: LIFE AND THOUGHT IN COLONIAL AMERICA

1. FIRST GREAT AWAKENING—early 18th-century wave of religious fervor that spread across all the colonies.
2. NEW LIGHT—emphasized an emotional approach to religious services.
3. FIRST GREAT AWAKENING—weakened the authority of Old Light Puritan ministers; led to the founding of new universities; increased the number of Protestant sects, thus promoting religious toleration.
4. FIRST GREAT AWAKENING—did NOT lead to efforts to emancipate slaves.
5. GEORGE WHITEFIELD—charismatic preacher associated with the First Great Awakening.
6. MERCANTILISM—economic policy designed to achieve a favorable balance of trade.
7. NAVIGATION ACTS—implemented British mercantile policies.
8. COLONIAL CITIES—mercantile centers; NOT linked by a system of rivers.
9. SALUTARY NEGLECT—period before 1763 in which the British did NOT enforce the Navigation Laws; promoted economic independence.
10. MARRIED WOMEN—had no separate legal identity apart from their husbands; colonial women were often midwives.
11. SLAVERY—began to dramatically increase in the late 17th century; legal in all 13 colonies.

12. DEISM—belief that natural laws regulate both the universe and human society.
13. BEN FRANKLIN—exemplified Enlightenment in America.
14. NATURAL RIGHTS—universal and inalienable rights that all governments must respect.
15. ZENGER CASE—established the principle that true statements about public figures cannot be prosecuted as libel, thus setting a precedent for freedom of the press.
16. COLONIAL TRANSPORTATION—sailing ships were the fastest mode of colonial transportation.
17. LITERACY OF NEW ENGLAND COLONISTS—the New England colonies boasted a very high literacy rate; this marked a significant cultural difference with the Southern colonies.

CHAPTER 6: SEVERING TIES WITH GREAT BRITAIN, 1754-1783

1. ALBANY PLAN OF UNION—proposed by Franklin to defend against French and Indian attacks; NOT adopted; but newspapers and pamphlets did facilitate and encourage colonial unity.
2. PEACE OF PARIS—France relinquished almost all of its New World empire to Great Britain.
3. PONTIAC'S REBELLION—Native Americans attempt to drive the British out of the trans-Appalachian region; NOT a slave rebellion.
4. PROCLAMATION LINE OF 1763—prompted by Pontiac's Rebellion; forbade colonists from crossing the Appalachian Mountains; widely ignored.
5. SUGAR ACT—first attempt to enforce the Navigation Acts; created custom duties.
6. STAMP ACT—enacted to raise revenue; instead raised the issue of Parliament's right to tax the colonies; thwarted by a colonial boycott of British goods; repealed by the Declaratory Act.
7. REPUBLICANISM—belief that government should be based on the consent of the governed.
8. BOSTON MASSACRE—depicted in a highly partisan engraving by Paul Revere.
9. INTOLERABLE ACTS—Parliament's response to the Boston Tea Party.
10. *COMMON SENSE*—influential pamphlet by Thomas Paine; castigated King George III as a "brute" and a "royal Pharaoh;" urged colonies to declare independence and establish a republic.

11. "REMEMBER THE LADIES"—Abigail Adams urges John Adams to extend republican rights to women.
12. DECLARATION OF INDEPENDENCE—begins with a list of inalienable rights; enumerates specific grievances against George III.
13. CONTINENTAL ARMY—ultimately organized like a highly disciplined European army; Washington understood that the Continental Army was an important symbol of Republicanism.
14. BATTLE OF SARATOGA—saved the New England colonies; led France to formally recognize the American colonies.
15. FRENCH AID—motivated by a desire for revenge against Great Britain; played a decisive role in the American victory.
16. PAPER CURRENCY—hampered the American war effort and led to unrest in the Continental Army.
17. TREATY OF PARIS—ended the War for Independence; established America's new boundaries.

CHAPTER 7: FORMING A NEW NATIONAL GOVERNMENT, 1781-1789

1. ARTICLES OF CONFEDERATION—America's first government; created a loose confederation; only a unicameral legislature; no judicial or executive branches; no power to tax.
2. NORTHWEST ORDINANCE of 1787—created orderly procedure for territories to become states; banned slavery; did NOT provide free land for settlers or financial compensation for Native Americans; Ohio was the first part of the Northwest Territory to become a state.
3. LOYALISTS—also called Tories; they did NOT refuse to lay down their arms and did NOT dominate the Second Continental Congress.
4. SHAYS' REBELLION—desperate farmers in western Massachusetts; demanded a halt in farm foreclosure and the printing of more paper money; did NOT try to overthrow the Massachusetts government; prompted colonial leaders to call for a stronger national government.
5. CONSTITUTION—built on a foundation of compromises.
6. FRAMERS—opposed political parties; believed a large republic would curb factionalism.
7. FEDERALISM—system of government in which a written constitution divides power between a central government and state governments.

8. GREAT COMPROMISE—resolved dispute between the large states and the small states; created a bicameral Congress; two senators per state.

9. THREE-FIFTHS COMPROMISE—indirectly acknowledges slavery; slaves count as three-fifths of a person for representation and taxation.

10. KEY PROVISIONS OF THE CONSTITUTION—bicameral Congress; separation of powers; checks and balances; Electoral College; "necessary and proper" clause; State of Union address, impeachment procedure.

11. NOT IN THE CONSTITUTION—a Bill of Rights; political parties, two-term limit for president; universal manhood suffrage; direct election of senators; Cabinet; right to a speedy trial.

12. ANTI-FEDERALISTS—opposed the Constitution; small farmers; feared a strong and potentially oppressive central government.

13. FEDERALISTS—supported the Constitution; merchants and large landowners; wanted a strong central government to protect property.

14. FEDERALIST PAPERS—written by Madison, Hamilton, and Jay to support ratification of the Constitution; Madison argued that a large republic would curb factionalism.

15. BILL OF RIGHTS—added after ratification of the Constitution; protected specific individual liberties; does NOT include the right of all citizens to vote.

CHAPTER 8: THE FEDERALIST ERA, 1789-1800

1. HAMILTON'S FINANCIAL PLAN—favored rich merchants and manufacturers; national debt is beneficial.

2. LOOSE CONSTRUCTIONIST—broad interpretation of the constitution; used by Hamilton to support his plan for a national bank.

3. STRICT CONSTRUCTIONIST—narrow interpretation of the constitution; used by Jefferson to oppose the National Bank.

4. HAMILTON AND JEFFERSON—both believed that America should be governed by an aristocracy of talent; disagreed the most over the constitutionality of the Bank of the United States.

5. WHISKEY REBELLION—sparked by an excise tax on the sale of whiskey; suppressed by Washington; demonstrated the power of the new federal government.

6. JAY'S TREATY—controversial, but did create a fragile peace with Great Britain.

7. WASHINGTON'S FAREWELL ADDRESS—avoid permanent alliances; contained similarities to aspects of the Monroe Doctrine; later used by opponents of the League of Nations and by isolationists.

8. ALIEN AND SEDITION ACTS—designed to silence Adams' critics.

9. KENTUCKY AND VIRGINIA RESOLUTIONS—written by Jefferson and Madison; formulated a STATES' RIGHTS doctrine; states can challenge and if necessary nullify federal laws.

CHAPTER 9: THE JEFFERSONIANS, 1801-1816

1. THE REVOLUTION OF 1800—peaceful transfer of power from the Federalists to the Jeffersonians; election signaled the end of the Federalist era.

2. JEFFERSONIAN DEMOCRACY—promoted Republican simplicity and the growth of an agrarian republic dominated by virtuous farmers.

3. LOUISIANA PURCHASE—doubled the size of the U.S.; purchase contradicted Jefferson's strict constructionist principles.

4. LEWIS AND CLARK EXPEDITION—strengthened American claims to the Pacific Northwest; did NOT explore the Hudson River.

5. THE EMBARGO OF 1807—unpopular with New England shippers; unforeseen effect of promoting American manufacturing; intended to maintain U.S. neutrality.

6. MARSHALL COURT—decisions supported a strong federal government and promoted business enterprise.

7. JUDICIAL REVIEW—gave the Supreme Court the authority to declare acts of Congress unconstitutional; established in *Marbury v. Madison*.

8. *MARBURY v. MADISON*—established the principle of judicial review; did NOT involve states' rights.

9. TECUMSEH AND TENSKWATAWA—charismatic Indian brothers who united tribes to oppose further U.S. expansion into the Old Northwest.

10. CAUSES OF THE WAR OF 1812—War Hawks hoped to annex Canada, safeguard the frontier, and defend American honor. War Hawks did NOT want to protect Native Americans.

11. CONSEQUENCES OF THE WAR OF 1812—promoted an increase in domestic manufacturing; intensified spirit of national unity; led to the demise of the Federalist Party; made Jackson a national hero; but did NOT result in any territorial gains.

CHAPTER 10: THE ERA OF GOOD FEELINGS, 1816-1824

1. JAMES MONROE—president during a period of national unity known as the Era of Good Feelings.
2. ADAMS–ONIS TREATY—gave both East and West Florida to the U.S.; defined the western boundary of the Louisiana Purchase.
3. MISSOURI COMPROMISE—maintained the Senate balance of power between slave and free states; admitted Missouri as a slave state and Maine as a free state; closed the remaining territory in the Louisiana Territory above 36°30' to slavery; viewed in the North as a "sacred pact;" criticized because it postponed the crisis over slavery.
4. MONROE DOCTRINE—unilateral declaration; Western Hemisphere is off limits to further European colonization; did NOT express a desire for the U.S. to form an alliance with Great Britain.
5. AMERICAN SYSTEM—promoted by Henry Clay; supported the national bank, tariffs, and internal improvements.
6. ERIE CANAL—lowered the cost of shipping between Buffalo and New York City; led to rapid growth of both cities; promoted commercial ties between Great Lake farmers and East Coast cities; did NOT raise prices.

CHAPTER 11: THE AGE OF JACKSON, 1824-1840

1. ELECTION OF JACKSON—reputation as a military hero played a key role in Jackson's election in 1828.
2. JACKSONIAN DEMOCRACY—champion of the common man; opponent of privileged elite; supporter of universal white male suffrage.
3. SPOILS SYSTEM—loyal party workers are rewarded with jobs; strongly endorsed by Jackson.
4. MAYSVILLE ROAD BILL—Jackson's veto provides a good example of strict constructionism.
5. BANK WAR—Jackson vetoed a bill to recharter the Second National Bank; veto played a key role in the creation of a new two-party system featuring the Whigs and the Democrats.

6. TARIFF OF ABOMINATIONS—created very high tariff rates; sparked outrage in the South.
7. DOCTRINE OF NULLIFICATION—advanced by John C. Calhoun of South Carolina; a state can nullify a federal law; based upon the doctrine of states' rights.
8. INDIAN REMOVAL ACT—Indians forced to exchange tribal lands in the East for government lands in the Indian Territory in Oklahoma.
9. *WORCESTER v. GEORGIA*—Marshall Court upholds the Cherokee Nation's right to their ancestral lands; not enforced by Jackson.
10. TRAIL OF TEARS—forcible evacuation of Cherokee; as many as one-fourth died along the 116-day forced march to the Indian Territory.
11. WHIGS—supported Clay and opposed Jackson.

CHAPTER 12: REFORM AND REFORMERS, 1800–1850

1. THE SECOND GREAT AWAKENING—wave of religious enthusiasm that spread across America in the early 1800s; Charles Grandison Finney was the best-known Second Great Awakening preacher; resulted in more women reformers.
2. BURNED-OVER DISTRICT—area in western New York where Finney and other preachers delivered "hellfire and damnation" sermons.
3. PERFECTIONISM—belief in the human ability to build a just society.
4. TRANSCENDENTALISM—philosophical and literary movement that stressed the importance of intuition and nonconformity; believed that truth could be found in nature.
5. LEADING TRANSCENDENTALISTS—Ralph Waldo Emerson, Henry David Thoreau, and Margaret Fuller were the leading Transcendentalists; Thoreau wrote *Walden*.
6. HUDSON RIVER SCHOOL—artists who painted landscapes that idealized the beauty of the American countryside.
7. ROMANTIC LITERATURE—looked to nature for insights and truth; Walt Whitman was America's leading Romantic poet.
8. UTOPIAN COMMUNITIES—tried to put the principles of Perfectionism into practice; Brook Farm and Oneida were the two best-known utopian communities.
9. DOROTHEA DIX—led a crusade to reform hospitals for the mentally ill.

10. HORACE MANN—leader in the movement to reform public education.
11. NATIVISM—anti-immigrant movement; focused on Catholic immigrants from Ireland and Germany; led to the formation of the Know-Nothing Party.
12. MORMONS—persecuted for practicing polygamy; moved west to Utah because of increased persecution; Brigham Young did NOT support women's rights.

CHAPTER 13: THE STRUGGLE FOR WOMEN'S RIGHTS, 1800-1850

1. STATUS OF MARRIED WOMEN—had no legal identity apart from their husbands.
2. REPUBLICAN MOTHERHOOD—women have a duty to raise their children to be virtuous citizens.
3. CULT OF DOMESTICITY—idealized women in their roles as wives and mothers.
4. LOWELL TEXTILE FACTORY—employed single women; created special supervised dormitories because the owners were originally concerned about the welfare of their employees: experiment ended when owners hired Irish immigrants.
5. SENECA FALLS CONVENTION—organized by Elizabeth Cady Stanton and Lucretia Mott; issued a Declaration of Sentiments calling for women's rights and the right to vote; did NOT call for equal pay for equal work or for birth control.
6. TEMPERANCE MOVEMENT—women played a key role; attempt to reduce the consumption of alcohol.

CHAPTER 14: THE COTTON KINGDOM, SLAVERY, AND THE FIRST ABOLITIONISTS, 1793-1860

1. TOBACCO—dominated the Southern economy during the colonial period.
2. COTTON GIN—revolutionized cotton production; made cotton America's most valuable cash crop.
3. COTTON AND SLAVERY—cotton tied the South to the institution of slavery; South argued that their "peculiar institution" was a "positive good" because they converted the slaves to Christianity.
4. WHITE SOCIETY IN THE OLD SOUTH—the majority of white families did NOT own any slaves; just one in four Southern families owned slaves.

5. SLAVE SOCIETY—slaves created a separate African American culture.

6. AMERICAN COLONIZATION SOCIETY—shipped freed slaves back to Africa; criticized for its gradual approach.

7. WILLIAM LLOYD GARRISON—published *The Liberator*; called for the immediate and unconditional abolition of all slaves.

8. GAG RULE—attempt by Southerners in the House of Representatives to table all antislavery resolutions without debate; later repealed.

9. FREDERICK DOUGLASS—foremost African American abolitionist.

CHAPTER 15: THE GATHERING STORM, 1836-1850

1. THE TEXAS ANNEXATION ISSUE—Jackson did not support the annexation of Texas because he feared it would trigger a divisive debate that would harm Van Buren's presidential election campaign.

2. MANIFEST DESTINY—belief that America was foreordained to extend its civilization across the North American continent; used by expansionists to justify the acquisition of Oregon; opposed by New England abolitionists.

3. JAMES K. POLK—ran on a platform demanding the annexation of Texas, the purchase of California, and the acquisition of all of Oregon.

4. FIFTY-FOUR FORTY OR FIGHT—slogan emphasizing America's willingness to fight for all of the Oregon Territory.

5. MEXICAN WAR—denounced by the Whigs and by New England abolitionists.

6. TREATY OF GUADALUPE HIDALGO—Mexico ceded New Mexico and California to the U.S.; the Gadsden Purchase was NOT part of the Treaty of Guadalupe Hidalgo; California was acquired as a result of the Mexican-American War.

7. WILMOT PROVISO—would prohibit slavery in all lands acquired from Mexico; blocked in the Senate.

8. THE COMPROMISE OF 1850—admitted California as a free state; abolished the slave trade in the District of Columbia; included a stringent Fugitive Slave Act; Lincoln was NOT involved in the negotiations; compromise did NOT recognize Kansas or Nebraska as states.

CHAPTER 16: THE NATION DIVIDES, 1850–1860

1. *UNCLE TOM'S CABIN*—intensified Northern opposition to slavery.
2. POPULAR SOVEREIGNTY—introduced by Stephen A. Douglas; settlers in a given territory have the right to decide whether or not to accept slavery; Kansas became the first test of popular sovereignty.
3. KANSAS-NEBRASKA ACT—repealed the Missouri Compromise ban on extending slavery into the Louisiana Territory; split the Democratic Party, led to the demise of the Whig Party and the rise of the Republican Party.
4. GADSDEN PURCHASE—Pierce administration purchased a strip of land in the Southwest to facilitate construction of a transcontinental railroad line; did NOT involve a loose versus strict interpretation of the Constitution.
5. DRED SCOTT DECISION—court ruled that Dred Scott was NOT a citizen; struck down the Northwest Ordinance and the Missouri Compromise; became a major issue in the Lincoln–Douglas debates.
6. JOHN BROWN'S RAID—intensified sectional bitterness; Brown became a martyr for the antislavery cause.
7. REPUBLICAN POSITION ON SLAVERY—the Republican Party platform accepted slavery in the states where it existed, but opposed any further extension of slavery into the new territories.
8. ELECTION OF 1860—Lincoln's election prompted South Carolina and six other Deep South states to secede from the Union.
9. CRITTENDEN COMPROMISE—final effort to save the Union; would extend the Missouri Compromise line across the entire country; rejected by Lincoln because the Republican platform opposed any extension of slavery.

CHAPTER 17: THE CIVIL WAR, 1861–1865

1. UNION STRENGTHS—large population and strong industrial base; Union did NOT have a supply of raw cotton.
2. REPUBLICAN-DOMINATED CONGRESS—did enact high tariffs, authorized a transcontinental railroad, a uniform national currency; did NOT abolish segregation, make high school mandatory, or grant government subsidies to industry.

3. MORRILL LAND GRANT ACT—stipulated that public lands be donated to states for providing colleges to train students in agriculture.

4. HOMESTEAD ACT—opened the Great Plains to settlers; supported the Republican ideal of "free soil, free land, free men."

5. SOUTHERN STRENGTHS—talented military commanders; supply of cotton.

6. SOUTHERN WEAKNESSES—did NOT have an extensive railroad network; did NOT effectively manage its economic resources.

7. BORDER STATES—Maryland and Kentucky were key border states that did NOT secede.

8. BATTLE OF VICKSBURG—gave the Union control of the Mississippi River.

9. BATTLE OF GETTYSBURG—Confederates crossed the Mason-Dixon line; Union victory prevented Lee from cutting off key rail links.

10. SHERMAN'S MARCH TO THE SEA—destroyed property and land in Georgia; crushed Southern morale.

11. EMANCIPATION PROCLAMATION—issued following the Union victory at Antietam; only freed slaves in Confederate states still in rebellion; did NOT free slaves in the border states.

12. NEW YORK CITY DRAFT RIOTS—Irish immigrants opposed the draft; complained that Civil War was " a rich man's war but a poor man's fight;" underscored racial, economic and cultural tensions in the North.

CHAPTER 18: RECONSTRUCTION AND THE OLD SOUTH, 1865-1900

1. THIRTEENTH AMENDMENT—abolished slavery; superseded the Emancipation Proclamation.

2. FOURTEENTH AMENDMENT—granted citizenship to the former slaves; negated the Dred Scott decision, forbade states from depriving any person of "life, liberty, or property without due process of law;" due process clause used to overturn Jim Crow segregation.

3. FIFTEENTH AMENDMENT—enfranchised African American males but did not grant the suffrage to women; opposed by many women's rights activists.

4. FREEDMAN'S BUREAU—created to help the newly freed slaves; did NOT encourage African Americans to migrate to the North.

5. IMPEACHMENT OF JOHNSON—Radical Republicans impeached Johnson for opposing their Reconstruction plans and for violating the Tenure of Office Act; Senate failed to convict Johnson by one vote.

6. CARPETBAGGERS—Northerners who headed South to seek power and profit.

7. SCALAWAGS—Southerners who betrayed the South by voting for the Republicans and by benefiting from Radical Republican policies.

8. BLACK CODES—limited the basic civil rights of the newly freed slaves.

9. SHARECROPPERS—newly freed slaves who exchanged their labor for the use of land, tools, and seed; created a cycle of debt and poverty.

10. EXODUSTERS—African Americans who left the South in the late 1870s to begin new lives in Kansas.

11. COMPROMISE OF 1877—Hayes agreed to withdraw Union troops from the South; ended Reconstruction.

12. *PLESSY v. FERGUSON*—Supreme Court rules that segregated railroad cars in Louisiana are legal; establishes the principle of "separate but equal;" overturned by *Brown v. Board of Education*.

13. BOOKER T. WASHINGTON—Atlanta Compromise speech urges African Americans to focus on vocational training and self-help.

14. W.E.B. Du BOIS—opposes Booker T. Washington's accomodationist views; advocates full economic, social, and political rights; calls upon the "talented tenth" to spearhead the fight for African American civil rights; one of the founders of the National Organization for Colored People (NAACP).

15. NEW SOUTH—New South leaders called Redeemers support economic diversity, but continue to enforce white supremacy.

CHAPTER 19: THE WEST, 1865-1900

1. MINERS—western mining camps contained a heterogeneous mix of people.

2. TRANSCONTINENTAL RAILROAD—built by Chinese and Irish workers; opened Great Plains to settlers; made it possible for hunters to destroy the buffalo herds.

3. CHISHOLM TRAIL—cattle trail stretching from San Antonio, Texas, to Abilene, Kansas.

SUPER FAST REVIEW

4. GREAT PLAINS AGRICULTURE—facilitated by barbed-wire fencing, wind-driven water pumps; iron plows, and reapers; chemical fertilizers were NOT used during the late 19th century.

5. *A CENTURY OF DISHONOR*—written by Helen Hunt Jackson; sharply criticized the government's treatment of Native Americans; mobilized support for the Dawes Severalty Act.

6. DAWES SEVERALTY ACT—intended to be a reform act to help the Plains Indians; harmed the Indians by dividing tribal lands into individual farms.

7. GHOST DANCE—ceremony designed to bring back the buffalo herds and cause the white settlers to leave.

8. TURNER FRONTIER THESIS—frontier experience played a key role in promoting democracy and individualism.

CHAPTER 20: INDUSTRY AND LABOR, 1865-1900

1. VERTICAL INTEGRATION—process by which a single company owns and controls the entire production process, from the unearthing of raw materials to the sale of finished products; used by Carnegie's steel company.

2. HORIZONTAL INTEGRATION—process by which a company gains control over other firms that produce the same product; used by Rockefeller and the Standard Oil Company.

3. TAYLORISM—system of scientific management developed by Frederick W. Taylor; based upon time-and-motion studies to eliminate wasted movements, reduce costs, and promote greater efficiency.

4. SOCIAL DARWINISM—belief that Darwin's theory of survival of the fittest can be applied to individuals, corporations, and nations.

5. GOSPEL OF WEALTH—Andrew Carnegie's belief that the rich have a responsibility to serve society by using their wealth to support worthy causes.

6. HORATIO ALGER—wrote popular novels describing how young boys succeeded through hard work, perseverance, and good luck.

7. KNIGHTS OF LABOR—open to all workers; initial rapid growth because of a few successful strikes and continuing industrialization of the U.S. economy; did NOT grow because of federal laws that protected labor's right to organize.

8. GREAT RAILROAD STRIKE OF 1877—first general strike in U.S. history; did NOT influence the American Federation of Labor (AFL).

9. HAYMARKET SQUARE RIOT—public outcry against unions hastened the decline of the Knights of Labor.

10. SAMUEL GOMPERS—leader of the American Federation of Labor (AFL); committed to craft unions of skilled workers; focused on "bread and butter" issues.

11. INDUSTRIAL WORKERS OF THE WORLD—tried to unite all workers; viewed conflict between labor and management as inevitable.

12. FEDERAL POLICIES TOWARD WORKERS—federal government called out troops to end strikes; did NOT promote retirement and workers' compensation programs.

13. SHERMAN ANTI-TRUST ACT—used to curb the power of labor unions.

14. THORSTEIN VEBLEN—criticized the lavish spending or "conspicuous consumption" of wealthy Americans during the Gilded Age.

15. THOMAS EDISON—created the first research laboratory in Menlo Park, New Jersey.

CHAPTER 21: URBAN LIFE AND CULTURE, 1865-1900

1. URBANIZATION—urban centers assumed a dominant role in American life; one in three Americans lived in urban areas by 1900.

2. CHICAGO—railroad center that became America's second largest city.

3. ELECTRIC TROLLEY CAR—promoted the growth of the first ring of suburbs.

4. MAIL-ORDER CATALOGUES—created a national retail market; standardized popular tastes, led to development of national advertising campaigns; hurt small-town merchants; did NOT lead to the decline of traditional big-city department stores.

5. THE NEW IMMIGRANTS—a massive wave of immigrants from Southern and Eastern Europe; settled in cities along the East Coast and in the Midwest.

6. NATIVISM—anti-foreign reaction; warned that the New Immigrants would not fully assimilate.

SUPER FAST REVIEW

7. THE CHINESE EXCLUSION ACT—prohibited Chinese workers from entering the U.S.; endorsed by residents of California, workers, and both political parties.

8. BIG CITY POLITICAL MACHINES—tightly organized groups of politicians who controlled the government in many American cities.

9. PATRONAGE—rewarding loyal party workers with political jobs.

10. SOCIAL GOSPEL—belief that America's churches have moral responsibility to take the lead in actively confronting social problems and helping the poor.

11. JANE ADDAMS—founded Hull House; leader of the settlement house movement; settlement houses provided opportunities for middle-class women to experience leadership positions.

12. ASHCAN SCHOOL OF ARTISTS—portrayed realistic scenes of urban life.

13. REALISTIC WRITERS—movement in American literature led by Stephen Crane and Theodore Dreiser; novels featured people caught in a web of social problems.

14. PRAGMATISM—emphasized factual knowledge and practical experience.

15. CLARA BARTON—founded the American Red Cross.

CHAPTER 22: THE POPULISTS AND THE PROGRESSIVES, 1880-1920

1. CAUSES OF FARM DISCONTENT—falling crop prices; discriminatory railroad rates; high tariff rates; deflationary money policy based upon the gold standard.

2. POPULIST PARTY PLATFORM—called for government control over the railroads; free coinage of silver; direct election of U.S. senators. Populists did NOT achieve their goal of the government taking control over the railroads.

3. INTERSTATE COMMERCE ACT—set important precedent as the first federal regulation of business and industry; ICA was regulatory, while the Sherman Anti-Trust Act was prohibitory.

4. WILLIAM JENNINGS BRYAN—delivered "Cross of Gold" speech; lost to McKinley in the 1896 presidential election.

5. *THE WONDERFUL WIZARD OF OZ*—political allegory on free silver and the plight of American farmers.

6. PROGRESSIVE SPIRIT—government should play an active role in solving social problems; competition will NOT inevitably improve society.

7. MUCKRAKERS—journalists who exposed corruption and social problems.
8. UPTON SINCLAIR—author of *The Jungle*; exposed unsanitary conditions in the meatpacking industry; prompted Congress to pass the Meat Inspection Act.
9. IDA TARBELL—wrote a critical history of the Standard Oil Company.
10. JACOB RIIS—photographs in *How the Other Side Lives* dramatized the plight of people living in New York City's Lower East Side.
11. JOHN DEWEY—leading educational philosopher who believed that children learn best by doing and experimenting.
12. NINETEENTH AMENDMENT—granted women the right to vote; Betty Friedan did NOT play a role in the fight to ratify the Nineteenth Amendment. Note that women's suffrage was first achieved in the Western states and then moved East.
13. WOMEN'S CHRISTIAN TEMPERANCE UNION—waged a successful fight to pass the Eighteenth Amendment banning the production and sale of alcoholic beverages.
14. SIXTEENTH AMENDMENT—gave Congress the power to lay and collect income taxes.
15. SEVENTEENTH AMENDMENT—provided that U.S. senators would be directly elected by voters in each state.
16. THEODORE ROOSEVELT—supported conservation; opposed "bad" trusts; intervened on behalf of labor in the United Mine Workers' strike; did NOT address issue of insider trading or ask Congress for an amendment granting women the right to vote.
17. BULL MOOSE PARTY—progressive third party founded and led by Theodore Roosevelt; split the Republican Party; key factor in Wilson's victory in the 1912 presidential election.
18. WOODROW WILSON—supported the Nineteenth Amendment granting women the right to vote.
19. PROGRESSIVES AND AFRICAN AMERICANS—Progressives did NOT work for laws banning the poll tax or literacy tests; Progressives were LEAST concerned about African American civil rights.
20. NATIONAL ASSOCIATION FOR THE ADVANCEMENT OF COLORED PEOPLE— founded in 1909 during the Progressive Era; used the courts to strike down Jim Crow laws.
21. IDA B. WELLS—principal public opponent of lynching in the South.

22. ARMORY SHOW—exposed Americans to Cubist paintings.
23. MAJOR LEAGUE BASEBALL—helped by rapid growth of cities.
24. SCOTT JOPLIN—leading African American composer of ragtime music.
25. MINSTREL SHOWS—lampooned African Americans as inferior, dim-witted, and superstitious.

CHAPTER 23: IMPERIALISM AND THE FIRST WORLD WAR, 1890-1919

1. ROOTS OF EXPANSIONISM—big business wanted new markets and new sources of raw materials; other expansionists believed that America had a responsibility to spread Christianity; acquiring new territories for America's expanding population was the LEAST used argument.
2. ALFRED T. MAHAN—author of *The Influence of Sea Power upon History*; argued for a strong navy, canal through Central America, and fueling stations in the Pacific.
3. OPEN DOOR POLICY—purpose was to protect American commercial interests in China.
4. CAUSES OF THE SPANISH-AMERICAN WAR—causes included "yellow journalism" and the sinking of the U.S.S. *Maine*.
5. CONSEQUENCES OF THE SPANISH-AMERICAN WAR—the U.S. acquired Puerto Rico and Philippines by force; marked first time U.S. acquired overseas territory by force; called "splendid little war" because it ended with a quick victory achieved with minimal cost; the citizens of Puerto Rico later became American citizens.
6. ANTI-IMPERIALISTS—opposed acquisition of the Philippines as contrary to the U.S. commitment to human freedom and self-determinism.
7. EMILIO AGUINALDO—Filipino resistance leader.
8. PANAMA CANAL—illustrated TR's "big stick" diplomacy.
9. ROOSEVELT COROLLARY—unilateral declaration that proclaimed a policing role for the U.S. in the Caribbean and Central America.
10. DOLLAR DIPLOMACY—Taft's policy of using American financial power to influence the foreign policy of Latin American countries and protect American business interests in these countries.

11. PANCHO VILLA—Mexican leader who raided the U.S. and provoked Wilson to retaliate by sending General Pershing into Mexico on a futile mission to find Villa; the raid hurt U.S.-Mexican relations.
12. SINKING OF THE *LUSITANIA*—highlighted the issue of freedom of the seas and prompted the U.S. to prepare for war.
13. ZIMMERMAN NOTE—tried to rekindle Mexican resentment over the loss of its territory in the Mexican-American War.
14. CENTRAL POWERS—when the U.S. entered World War I the Central Powers included Germany, Austria-Hungary, the Ottoman Empire, and Bulgaria.
15. GREAT MIGRATION—mass movement of African Americans from the rural South to urban centers in the North and Midwest; triggered by the wartime demand for labor.
16. COMMITTEE OF PUBLIC INFORMATION—mobilized public support for the war effort.
17. ESPIONAGE ACT – criticized for threatening to take away fundamental freedoms guaranteed by the Bill of Rights.
18. FOURTEEN POINTS—included open diplomacy, freedom of the seas, partial disarmament, and self-determination; did NOT include creating an International Monetary Fund, entering secret alliances, recognizing the Soviet Union, creating a global currency, or recognizing the right to individualism.
19. TREATY OF VERSAILLES—Wilson's prime objective was for the treaty to include a charter for the League of Nations; did NOT include a provision calling for the disarmament of ALL great powers.
20. LEAGUE OF NATIONS—Senate opponents argued that the League would limit American sovereignty and violate Washington's admonition to avoid entangling alliances; the Senate never approved the Treaty of Versailles, and the United States never joined the League of Nations.

CHAPTER 24: THE ROARING TWENTIES, 1919-1929

1. RED SCARE—widespread fear of Communists and aliens immediately following the First World War.
2. PALMER RAIDS—part of the Red Scare; several thousand alleged radicals arrested.
3. SACCO AND VANZETTI CASE—illustrated the nation's fear of radicals and recent immigrants.

4. NATIONAL ORIGINS ACT OF 1924—established immigration quotas for each national group; severely limited immigration from Southern and Eastern Europe.

5. SCOPES TRIAL—tested the legality of teaching evolution; illustrated a growing cultural conflict between modernism (science) and fundamentalism (religion).

6. *THE BIRTH OF A NATION*—film glamorizing the KKK.

7. GREAT MIGRATION— movement of African Americans from the rural South to cities in the North continued.

8. HARLEM RENAISSANCE—outpouring of African American literary and artistic creativity that flourished in Harlem during the 1920s; leading members included Langston Hughes, Jean Toomer, James Weldon Jones, Claude McKay, and Zora Neale Hurston; A. Philip Randolph was NOT a member.

9. MARCUS GARVEY—major African American leader during the 1920s; emphasized Black pride and Pan-Africanism.

10. JAZZ—identified with Roaring Twenties; represented a break with tradition; Billie Holiday was a popular jazz singer and "Duke" Ellington was a popular big band leader; first truly American art.

11. FLAPPERS—modern women who challenged traditional codes of dress and behavior.

12. MARGARET SANGER—advocated birth control.

13. LOST GENERATION—writers who criticized middle-class materialism and conformity; many members became expatriates living in Paris; leading members included F. Scott Fitzgerald, Sinclair Lewis, and Ernest Hemingway.

14. ERNEST HEMINGWAY—Lost Generation writer; *A Farewell to Arms* was NOT about Reconstruction; *The Sun Also Rises* was NOT about baby boomers.

15. HARDING, COOLIDGE, AND HOOVER—Republican presidents; all supported lower taxes for the wealthy, high tariffs, and lax enforcement of anti-trust laws.

16. TEAPOT DOME SCANDAL – involved the secret leasing of oil reserves to private corporations; occurred during the Harding administration.

17. WASHINGTON DISARMAMENT CONFERENCE—established ratios for the construction of battleships and aircraft carriers.

18. DAWES PLAN—U.S. loans to Germany.

19. HENRY FORD—successfully applied the principles of a moving assembly line to the manufacture of automobiles.

CHAPTER 25: THE GREAT DEPRESSION AND THE NEW DEAL, 1929-1941

1. CAUSES OF THE GREAT DEPRESSION—declining farm prices, overproduction by business, and under-consumption by consumers; the Great Depression was NOT caused by excessive government regulation; period of deflation, NOT inflation.
2. HOOVERVILLE—sarcastic term for shantytowns inhabited by unemployed and homeless people.
3. DUST BOWL—drought-stricken area centered in Oklahoma, Kansas, and Colorado; depicted in Hogue's painting "Drought Stricken Area."
4. *THE GRAPES OF WRATH*—by John Steinbeck; vivid description of the plight of Okies migrating to California.
5. DOROTHEA LANGE—photographs publicized the plight of migrant farm workers.
6. RECONSTRUCTION FINANCE CORPORATION—supported by Hoover; provided federal loans to banks.
7. BONUS MARCH—World War I veterans lobbed Congress for early payment of their war bonus; Congress refused; Hoover sent army to breakup the Bonus encampment in Washington; similar to Coxey's Army in 1894.
8. NEW DEAL—pragmatic program of relief, recovery, and reform; intended to reform the capitalist system; did NOT nationalize the banks, restructure the courts, or include the Lend-Lease program.
9. DEFICIT SPENDING—federal government spends more money than it takes in; intended to stimulate the economy.
10. CIVILIAN CONSERVATION CORPS—provided conservation jobs for unemployed youth.
11. AGRICULTURAL ADJUSTMENT ACT—reduce farm surpluses by decreasing the amount of land under cultivation; struck down by the Supreme Court.
12. SECURITIES EXCHANGE COMMISSION—agency to regulate the stock market.
13. TENNESSEE VALLEY AUTHORITY—long-term program; series of dams to prevent floods and provide cheap electricity.
14. WORKS PROJECTS ADMINISTRATION—provided jobs for unemployed artists and writers.

15. NATIONAL RECOVERY ACT—businesses create codes of fair competition; symbol was a Blue Eagle; struck down by the Supreme Court.

16. INDIAN REORGANIZATION ACT—reverses Dawes Severalty Act.

17. SOCIAL SECURITY ACT—most far-reaching New Deal program; now threatened by retiring Baby Boomers.

18. FATHER COUGLIN—"radio priest" and leading New Deal critic.

19. WAGNER ACT—also known as the National Labor Relations Act; guaranteed workers the right to organize and bargain collectively.

20. JOHN L. LEWIS—important labor leader who formed the Congress of Industrial Organization (CIO) to organized unskilled workers in major industries.

21. NEW DEAL AND AFRICAN AMERICANS—New Deal programs did NOT directly confront racial injustice; African Americans did benefit from New Deal programs; African Americans switched their allegiance to the Democratic Party.

22. ELEANOR ROOSEVELT—most visible champion of women's rights during the New Deal era.

23. COURT-PACKING PLAN—Supreme Court struck down the National Recovery Act and the Agricultural Adjustment Act; FDR wanted to increase the number of justices; seen as a violation of judicial independence and the separation of powers; NOT enacted.

24. NEW DEAL AND THE DEPRESSION—the New Deal did NOT end the Great Depression.

CHAPTER 26: THE SECOND WORLD WAR, 1931-1945

1. NYE COMMITTEE—concluded that greedy corporations lured America into the First World War to make a profit; supported Neutrality Acts.

2. ISOLATIONISM—U.S. should avoid making political commitments to other nations; influenced by Washington's Farewell Address.

3. STIMSON DOCTRINE—U.S. refuses to recognize Japanese conquest of Manchuria; ignored by the Japanese.

4. GOOD NEIGHBOR POLICY—U.S. renounces the Roosevelt Corollary; created reciprocal trade agreements; created united hemispheric front against fascism.

5. LEND-LEASE—U.S. becomes the "arsenal of democracy;" provides massive military aid to Great Britain and Russia.
6. PEARL HARBOR—ended U.S. neutrality.
7. BIG THREE—FDR, Churchill, and Stalin; agree on a strategy to defeat Hitler first; demand unconditional surrender of Germany and Italy.
8. JAMES B. BYRNE—Secretary of State under Truman; papers are important record of diplomatic events at end of World War II.
9. DOUBLE V CAMPAIGN—African American soldiers fight in segregated units; African Americans will fight against fascism abroad and for democracy at home.
10. ROSIE THE RIVETER—fictional symbol of working women during World War II.
11. ZOOT SUIT RIOTS—baggy clothes worn by Mexican American youth in Los Angeles; sailors and soldiers stationed in Los Angeles accuse youth of being unpatriotic; tensions escalate into riots that last a week.
12. INTERNMENT OF JAPANESE AMERICANS—War Relocation Authority relocates Japanese Americans into detention camps; most serious violation of civil liberties in wartime in U.S. history.
13. *KOREMATSU v. UNITED STATES*—Supreme Court upholds the constitutionality of the Japanese interment program.
14. PERSUASION POSTERS – used to persuade people to support the war effort; appealed to patriotism; the "United We Win" campaign fought racial discrimination; the "Waste Helps the Enemy" urged people to practice home front conservation.
15. MANHATTAN PROJECT—top secret project to build an atomic bomb; U.S. arsenal only contained two bombs.
16. DECISION TO USE ATOMIC BOMB—Truman was NOT influenced by public opinion, since the existence of the atomic bomb was a secret; Truman wanted to save American lives, force the Japanese to surrender, and convince Stalin to be more cooperative.

CHAPTER 27: TRUMAN AND THE COLD WAR, 1945-1952

1. IRON CURTAIN SPEECH—Churchill warned that Stalin was transforming Eastern Europe into a Soviet sphere of influence.
2. GEORGE KENNAN—father of containment.
3. CONTAINMENT—strategic policy of blocking Soviet expansion.

4. TRUMAN DOCTRINE—Truman's pledge to use American power to support "free peoples" who resist Communist subversion; first used to aid Greece and Turkey.

5. MARSHALL PLAN—program of economic aid to assist Western European nations in recovery from World War II; this recovery would thwart the growth of Communist political parties.

6. UNITED NATIONS—designed to promote international peace; NOT intended to curb the power of the Soviet Union.

7. NATO—based upon the principle of collective security.

8. BERLIN BLOCKADE—Soviet attempt to drive the Allies out of West Berlin

9. BERLIN AIRLIFT—successful use of Allied air power to overcome Soviet land blockade by airlifting food and fuel into West Berlin.

10. FALL OF CHINA—U.S. refused to recognize Mao's new government in Beijing; heightened anticommunist hysteria in U.S.; U.S. recognized the government in Taiwan as representative of all of China.

11. KOREAN WAR—precipitated by North Korean invasion of South Korea; marked first use of collective military action by United Nations; ended by an armistice or cease-fire which left the boundaries at almost the same place as when the war started; first conflict in which American soldiers fought in integrated military units; U.S. did NOT become bogged down in a guerilla war.

12. GENERAL MacARTHUR—fired for insubordination.

CHAPTER 28: DOMESTIC DEVELOPMENTS DURING THE TRUMAN YEARS, 1945-1952

1. MOVIES ABOUT ALIEN INVADERS—reflected Cold War anxieties.

2. RICHARD NIXON, JOHN F. KENNEDY, AND JOSEPH McCARTHY—all launched their political careers as strong anticommunists.

3. McCARTHYISM—unsubstantiated accusations of disloyalty without evidence; political climate of paranoia associated with the perceived threat of communist subversion in the United States; targeted Communists and Communist sympathizers.

4. HOLLYWOOD BLACKLIST—list of writers, directors, and actors suspended from work because of suspected left-wing political beliefs.

5. FALL OF McCARTHY—his bullying tactics during the televised Army-McCarthy hearings turned public opinion against him.
6. FAIR DEAL—Truman's program of social and economic reforms; did NOT include plans to nationalize basic industries.
7. TAFT-HARTLEY ACT—designed to curb the power of labor unions; strongly supported by the business community.
8. DIXIECRATS—Southern segregationists, led by Strom Thurmond, who left the Democratic Party in the 1948 presidential election.
9. TRUMAN—issued executive order that desegregated the armed forces; U.S. forces fought Korean War in integrated units.

CHAPTER 29: THE 1950s

1. MASSIVE RETALIATION—Eisenhower–Dulles strategic policy of a willingness to use nuclear weapons to halt Communist aggression.
2. BRINKSMANSHIP—willingness to go to the brink of nuclear war.
3. SPUTNIK—Soviet satellite that orbited the Earth; prompted Congress to create NASA and enact the National Defense Education Act to fund accelerated science and math programs.
4. SUEZ CRISIS—successfully mediated by Eisenhower.
5. MILITARY-INDUSTRIAL COMPLEX—contributed to America's economic growth; Eisenhower warned that it could pose a threat to American democracy.
6. WILLIAM LEVITT—applied assembly-line production techniques to building homes in communities often called Levitt Towns.
7. GI BILL—provided veterans with bargain mortgages and college tuition; did NOT provide loans for cars.
8. FEDERAL HIGHWAY ACT OF 1956—enacted during the Eisenhower administration: funded the construction of the interstate highway system.
9. NEW CULT OF DOMESTICITY—return to traditional gender roles following World War II; particularly prevalent in suburbs.
10. *THE HONEYMOONERS, DAVY CROCKETT,* AND *THE MICKEY MOUSE CLUB*—popular television programs that reflected aspects of popular culture in the 1950s.
11. JAMES DEAN AND MARLON BRANDO – popular actors who dramatized youthful rebellion.
12. *THE LONELY CROWD* AND *THE MAN IN THE GRAY FLANNEL SUIT*—books that criticized conformity during the 1950s.

13. BEAT GENERATION—name given to 1950s rebels who rejected excessive materialism and mindless conformity of American life.

14. JACK KEROUAC—best-known Beat Generation author; wrote *On the Road*; reflected alienation felt by the Beat Generation.

15. EDWARD HOPPER—known for paintings that captured the isolation and alienation of American life.

16. JACKSON POLLOCK—known for Abstract Expressionist paintings that lack recognizable subjects.

CHAPTER 30: THE CIVIL RIGHTS MOVEMENT, 1954-1960

1. DOUBLE V CAMPAIGN—called for African Americans to fight for victory against fascism in Europe and victory against racism in America.

2. NAACP—followed a strategy of using the courts to overturn Jim Crow segregation laws.

3. *BROWN v. BOARD OF EDUCATION*—struck down the "separate but equal doctrine" established in *Plessy v. Ferguson*; used the equal protection clause of the Fourteenth Amendment to rule that separate but equal public schools were unconstitutional.

4. LITTLE ROCK—President Eisenhower sent federal troops to enforce the local court-ordered desegregation plan.

5. DR. MARTIN LUTHER KING JR.—catapulted to national fame by the Montgomery Bus Boycott; championed a strategy of nonviolent civil disobedience; influenced by the writings of Henry David Thoreau and the teachings of Gandhi.

6. SOUTHERN CHRISTIAN LEADERSHIP CONFERENCE (SCLC)— Civil rights organization founded and led by Dr. King.

7. SIT-IN MOVEMENT—began as student-led protests against segregated lunch counters; implemented Dr. King's strategy of nonviolent civil disobedience.

8. STUDENT NONVIOLENT COORDINATING COMMITTEE (SNCC)—formed to facilitate student activism.

CHAPTER 31: THE TUMULTUOUS SIXTIES–PART I

1. JOHN F. KENNEDY—America's first Roman Catholic president.

2. TELEVISED PRESIDENTIAL DEBATES—played a key role in convincing voters that JFK was ready to become president.

3. CAMELOT—popular name given to Kennedy administration.

4. PEACE CORPS—most popular New Frontier program.

5. BAY OF PIGS INVASION—intended to overthrow Castro; fiasco that damaged JFK's credibility.

6. CUBAN MISSILE CRISIS—resolved when Khrushchev agreed to remove Soviet missiles from Cuba in exchange for an American pledge to not invade Cuba and overthrow Castro.

7. FREEDOM RIDERS—white and black volunteers who tested Southern compliance with Court decisions ordering the desegregation of interstate buses and public facilities at bus terminals.

8. "LETTER FROM BIRMINGHAM JAIL"—Dr. King's defense of nonviolent civil disobedience to protest unjust segregation laws.

9. MARCH ON WASHINGTON—marked the historic moment when the civil rights movement achieved its greatest unity.

10. CIVIL RIGHTS ACT OF 1964—barred discrimination in public facilities; outlawed discrimination in employment based upon race, creed, national origins, and sex; LBJ used the assassination of President Kennedy to mobilize support for the act.

11. MISSISSIPPI FREEDOM SUMMER—campaign to register black voters in Mississippi.

12. VOTING RIGHTS ACT OF 1965—outlawed literacy tests and other tactics used to prevent blacks from voting.

13. TWENTY-FOURTH AMENDMENT—outlawed the poll tax.

14. GREAT SOCIETY—name given to LBJ's legislative program; included Medicare and Medicaid, a War on Poverty, urban renewal, job training, and funds for education.

15. NOT PART OF THE GREAT SOCIETY—did NOT guarantee full employment, establish the Peace Corps, or create Social Security.

16. IMMIGRATION ACT OF 1965—ended the system of national origins quotas created during the 1920s; led to a significant increase in immigration from Latin America and Asia.

17. THE GREAT SOCIETY AND THE NEW DEAL—both included programs to promote the arts, help the elderly, encourage housing construction, raise employment levels, and reduce poverty. The New Deal did NOT include programs specifically designed to protect the civil rights of African Americans.

18. *MIRANDA v. ARIZONA*—police must inform arrested persons of their constitutional rights.

19. *BAKER v. CARR*—established principle of "one man, one vote."

CHAPTER 32: THE TUMULTUOUS SIXTIES–PART II

1. INDOCHINA—the U.S. replaced France as the leading Western power in Indochina; France unsuccessfully appealed to President Eisenhower for bombers to help relieve the siege of Dien Bien Phu.

2. DOMINO THEORY—used to justify America's support for South Vietnam.

3. TONKIN GULF RESOLUTION—based upon unsubstantiated reports of an alleged North Vietnamese attack on U.S. warships in the Gulf of Tonkin; gave President Johnson a blank check to escalate the war in Vietnam.

4. HAWKS—supported the Vietnam War.

5. DOVES—opposed the Vietnam War.

6. TET OFFENSIVE—triggered widespread domestic dissent in the U.S.; forced LBJ to withdraw from the 1968 presidential election.

7. MALCOLM X—charismatic Black Muslin leader who preached a philosophy of militant black separatism.

8. STOKELY CARMICHAEL—new leader of SNCC; best known for championing BLACK POWER.

9. BLACK POWER—blacks should build economic and political power by forming black-owned businesses and voting for black candidates.

10. BETTY FRIEDAN—author of *The Feminist Mystique*; one of the founders of the National Organization for Women (NOW); helped spark the women's rights movement.

11. RACHEL CARSON—author of *Silent Spring*; called for a ban on DDT; helped galvanize American environmental movement.

12. THREE MILE ISLAND—nuclear power plant in Pennsylvania; an accident in the plant raised public concerns about the safety of nuclear power.

13. RALPH NADER—author of *Unsafe at Any Speed*; leader of the consumer rights movement; also called attention to the problem of nuclear waste.

14. ANDY WARHOL—America's most famous Pop artist; best known for his pop portraits of Campbell soup cans.

CHAPTER 33: THE 1970s–NIXON, CARTER, AND THE AGE OF LIMITS

1. VIETNAMIZATION—President Nixon's policy of training South Vietnamese soldiers to take over military responsibilities from American troops.

2. SILENT MAJORITY—President Nixon used this term to describe hard-working Americans who supported his policies in Vietnam. The Silent Majority typically included white middle-class Americans who often lived in fast-growing states in the South and West.

3. INVASION OF CAMBODIA—Nixon ordered American troops to invade Cambodia to cut North Vietnamese supply lines into South Vietnam.

4. KENT STATE—the Cambodian invasion triggered widespread student demonstrations on campuses across America. National Guard soldiers killed four students at Kent State University in Ohio.

5. PARIS ACCORDS—peace agreement that ended America's military involvement in the Vietnam War.

6. WAR POWERS ACT—restricted the president's ability to unilaterally deploy troops into war zones without congressional approval.

7. VIETNAM SYNDROME—skepticism about military involvements that might become another "Vietnam."

8. RELATIONS WITH CHINA—Nixon became the first American president to visit China.

9. DÉTENTE—Nixon's policy of relaxing tensions with the Soviet Union. Examples of détente include the SALT I treaty and Nixon's visit to Moscow.

10. ARAB OIL EMBARGO—marked the end of America's post-war economic boom.

11. IMPEACHMENT OF NIXON—the House Judiciary Committee voted to recommend the impeachment of President Nixon for obstruction of justice. This provides an example of the process of checks and balances.

12. INFLATION—President Ford's most pressing problem.

13. CAUSES OF INFLATION—soaring energy costs, the federal deficit, rising health care costs, and the high cost of the Vietnam War.

14. STAGFLATION—the combination of high inflation and high unemployment that affected the U.S. economy during most of the 1970s.
15. HUMAN RIGHTS—the primary foreign policy goal of the Carter administration.
16. CAMP DAVID ACCORDS—peace agreement between Egypt and Israel; high point of the Carter presidency.
17. IRANIAN HOSTAGE CRISIS—damaged Carter's approval ratings.
18. *ROE v. WADE*—upheld abortion rights for women.
19. *REGENTS OF THE UNIVERSITY OF CALIFORNIA v. BAKKE*— Struck down rigid affirmative action quotas; also ruled that race could be used as one factor in admission decisions.

CHAPTER 34: KEY EVENTS AND TRENDS, 1980–PRESENT

1. BARRY GOLDWATER—conservative senator from Arizona who ran for president in 1964; supported by states' rights proponents.
2. MORAL MAJORITY—founded and led by Jerry Falwell; believed that permissive policies were eroding core American family values.
3. NEW RIGHT—conservative coalition that supported Reagan, emphasized patriotism, and stressed family values.
4. REAGANOMICS—Reagan's economic program to promote growth and investment by cutting taxes and deregulating business; also called supply-side economics.
5. REAGAN DOCTRINE—Reagan's strategy to confront and oppose the global influence of the Soviet Union.
6. STAR WARS—anti-missile program to defend the United States; critics accused Reagan of spending too much money on an unrealistic program.
7. MIKHAIL GORBACHEV—Soviet leader who initiated a major reform program that included relaxing controls over Eastern Europe.
8. PURPOSE OF PERSIAN GULF WAR—to liberate Kuwait.
9. NAFTA—created a free-trade zone with Canada and Mexico; created during the Clinton presidency.
10. WTO—established during the Clinton presidency to oversee trade agreements and enforce trade rules.
11. NEWT GINGRICH—Republican Speaker of the House who often thwarted Clinton's legislative program.

12. IMPEACHMENT OF CLINTON—impeached by the House for perjury and obstruction of justice.
13. WEAPONS OF MASS DESTRUCTION – used by the Bush administration to justify the war with Iraq.
14. ATTACK ON AFGHANISTAN—immediately followed the 9/11 attacks; preceded the invasion of Iraq.
15. BABY BOOMERS—76 million Americans born between 1946 and 1964; now pose a threat to the solvency of the Social Security system.
16. SUNBELT—band of fast-growing states that stretch from the Carolinas to Southern California.
17. NEW WAVE OF IMMIGRANTS—largest number are coming from Latin America and Asia.
18. EQUAL RIGHTS AMENDMENT—was NOT ratified by the states and thus is NOT part of the Constitution.
19. PHYLLIS SCHLAFLY—led the successful opposition to the Equal Rights Amendment.
20. GERALDINE FERRARO—first female vice-presidential candidate; ran on the 1984 Democratic ticket with Walter Mondale.
21. KEY TRENDS FOR WOMEN—continued to enter the labor force in record numbers; more and more women entered professional jobs, still earning less than men; increasing numbers of women attended college and graduate school.
22. DISCO – a popular dance and music genre often associated with the Gay Rights movement.

SUPER FAST REVIEW

—PART 3—

KEY
QUOTES
YOU ABSOLUTELY,
POSITIVELY HAVE
TO KNOW

1. **Christopher Columbus reveals a totally ethnocentric attitude toward learning about the customs of Native Americans, 1492:**

   "It appears to me, that the people are ingenious and would be good servants; and I am of the opinion that they would very readily become Christians, as they appear to have no religion. They very quickly learn such words as are spoken to them. If it please our Lord, I intend on my return to carry home six of them to your Highnesses, that they may learn our language."

2. **John Winthrop urges the Puritans to build a model Christian community, 1630:**

   "For we must consider that we shall be as city upon a hill. The eyes of all people are upon us. So that if we shall deal falsely with our God in this work we have undertaken, and so cause Him to withdraw His present help from us, we shall be made a story and a by-word through the world."

3. **Jonathan Edwards warns his congregation in this famous First Great Awakening sermon known as "Sinners in the Hands of an Angry God," 1741:**

   "The God that holds you over the pit of hell, much as one holds a spider, or some loathsome insect over the fire, abhors you, and is dreadfully provoked: his wrath towards you burns like fire; he looks upon you as worthy of nothing else, but to be cast into the fire; he is of purer eyes than to bear to have you in his sight; you are ten thousand times more abominable in his eyes, than the most hateful venomous serpent is in ours."

KEY QUOTES

4. Benjamin Franklin opens his *Autobiography*, 1771:

"Imagining it may be equally agreeable to you to know the circumstances of my life, many of which you are yet unacquainted with, and expecting the enjoyment of a week's uninterrupted leisure in my present country retirement, I sit down to write them for you. To which I have besides some other inducements. Having emerged from the poverty and obscurity in which I was born and bred, to a state of affluence and some degree of reputation in the world, and having gone so far through life with a considerable share of felicity, the conducing means I made use of, which, with the blessing of God, so well succeeded, my posterity may like to know, as they may find some of them suitable to their own situations, and therefore fit to be imitated."

5. Thomas Paine challenges the authority of King George III in this passage from *Common Sense*, 1776:

"No man was a warmer wisher for reconciliation than myself, before the fatal nineteenth of April 1775, but the moment the event of that day was made known, I rejected the hardened, sullen tempered Pharaoh of England for ever; and disdain the wretch, that with the pretended title of FATHER OF HIS PEOPLE, can unfeelingly hear of their slaughter, and composedly sleep with their blood upon his soul."

6. Abigail Adams urges her husband, John Adams, to support greater rights for women, 1776:

"In the new Code of Laws which I suppose it will be necessary for you to make I desire you would Remember the Ladies and be more generous and favourable to them than your ancestors. Do not put such unlimited power into the hands of the Husbands. Remember all Men would be tyrants if they could."

7. **James Madison argues that a large republic would curb factionalism, 1787:**

   "In an expanding Republic, so many different groups and viewpoints would be included in the Congress that tyranny by the majority would be impossible."

8. **James Madison argues in The Federalist No. 51 that the structure of the new government must provide proper checks and balances among the different branches of government, 1788:**

   "Ambition must be made to counteract ambition... If men were angels, no government would be necessary. If angels were to govern men, neither external nor internal controls on government would be necessary. In framing a government which is to be administered by men over men, the great difficulty lies in this: you must first enable the government to control the governed; and then in the next place oblige it to control itself."

9. **Patrick Henry asked this question during the Virginia ratification debate, 1788. John C. Calhoun would have answered "Yes," because he was a supporter of states' rights.**

   "Is this a confederacy, like Holland—an association of a number of independent states, each of which retains its individual sovereignty?"

10. **Alexander Hamilton advocating the value of a national debt, 1789:**

    "A national debt if it is not excessive will be to us a national blessing, it will be a powerful cement of our union."

KEY QUOTES

11. **Alexander Hamilton explaining that the "necessary and proper" clause can be used to justify the creation of a national bank, 1790:**

   "To make all laws which shall be necessary and proper for carrying into execution the foregoing powers, and all other power vested by this Constitution."

12. **George Washington using his Farewell Address to admonish Americans to avoid entangling foreign alliances, 1796. It is important to note the similarity between Washington's Farewell Address and the Monroe Doctrine. It is also important to note that during the 1930s isolationists used the Farewell Address to support the neutrality laws.**

   "The great rule of conduct for us in regard to foreign nations is, in extending our commercial relations, to have with them as little political connection as possible. So far as we have already formed engagements, let them be fulfilled with perfect good faith. Here let us stop."

13. **Thomas Jefferson stating that a constitutional amendment will ultimately be needed to make the Louisiana Purchase legal, 1803:**

   "This treaty must of course be laid before both Houses, because both have important functions to exercise respecting it. They, I presume, will see their duty to their country in ratifying and paying for it, so as to secure a goal which would otherwise probably be never again in their power. But I suppose they must then appeal to the nation for an additional article to the Constitution, approving and confirming an act which the nation had not previously authorized."

14. **Andrew Jackson asserting his belief that Native Americans lack legal status as sovereign nations, 1817:**

   "I have long viewed treaties with American Indians as an absurdity not to be reconciled to the principles of our government."

15. **Reginald Heber's famous hymn expressing Protestant missionary goals, 1819:**

   "From Greenland's icy mountains,
   From India's coral strand;
   Where Africa's sunny fountains
   Roll down their golden sand;
   From many an ancient river,
   From many a palmy plain,
   They call us to deliver
   Their land from error's chain."

16. **Thomas Jefferson discusses slavery, the Missouri question, and the overall dilemma posed by slavery, 1820:**

   "But, as it is, we have the wolf by the ear, and we can neither hold him, nor safely let him go. Justice is in one scale, and self-preservation in the other."

KEY QUOTES

17. James Monroe issuing his famous unilateral declaration of principles that later became known as the Monroe Doctrine, 1823:

"Any country whose people conduct themselves well can count upon our hearty friendship. If a nation shows that it knows how to act with reasonable efficiency and decency in social and political matters, if it keeps order and pays its obligations, it need fear no interference from the United States. Chronic wrongdoing, or an impotence which results in a general loosening of the ties of civilized society, may in America, as elsewhere, ultimately require intervention by some civilized nation, and in the Western Hemisphere the adherence of the United States to the Monroe Doctrine may force the United States, however reluctantly, in flagrant cases of such wrongdoing or impotence, to the exercise of an international police power."

"It is impossible that the allied powers should extend their political system to any portion of either continent, without endangering our peace and happiness: nor can any one believe that our Southern Brethren, if left to themselves, would adopt it of their own accord. It is equally impossible, therefore, that we should behold such interposition, in any form, with indifference."

18. Robert Owen declaring his intention to found a new utopian community in the United States, 1826:

"I have come to this country to introduce an entire new state of society; to change it from an ignorant, selfish system to an enlightened social system which shall gradually unite all interests into one and remove all causes for contest between individuals."

19. **John C. Calhoun issues the Ordinance of Nullification declaring federal duties imposts on foreign goods to be "null and void" in South Carolina, 1832:**

"We, therefore,...do declare and ordain,...That the several acts...are unauthorized by the Constitution of the United States...and are null, void, and no law, nor binding upon this State, its officers or citizens."

20. **Andrew Jackson declaring his intention to ignore the Supreme Court ruling in favor of Native Americans in *Worcester v. Georgia*, 1832:**

"John Marshall has made his decision; now let him enforce it!"

21. **Sarah Moore Grimké expresses her strongly held view of women's rights, 1837:**

"I ask no favors for my sex.... All I ask of our brethren is that they will take their feet from off our necks. "

22. **Catharine Beecher explains the important role that women play in terms of the cult of domesticity, 1837:**

"The mother writes the character of the future man; the sister bends the fibres that hereafter are the forest tree; the wife sways the heart, whose energies may turn for good or for evil the destinies of a nation. Let the women of a country be virtuous and intelligent, and the men will certainly be the same."

23. **Ralph Waldo Emerson defines the core beliefs of Transcendentalism, 1841:**

"To believe your own thought, to believe that what is true for you in your private heart is true for all men,—that is genius." "The height, the deity of man is to be self-sustained, to need no gift, no foreign force. Society is good when it does not violate me, but best when it is likest to solitude."

KEY QUOTES

24. The editors of the Democratic Review express their belief in the inevitability of manifest destiny, 1845:

"Texas has been absorbed into the Union in the inevitable fulfillment of the general law which is rolling our population westward... It was disintegrated from Mexico in the natural course of events, by a process perfectly legitimate on its own part, blameless on ours... Its incorporation into the Union was not only inevitable, but the most natural, right and proper thing in the world."

25. John L. O'Sullivan expresses his conviction that America has a "manifest destiny" to extend its civilization across the continent, 1845:

"By the right of our manifest destiny to overspread and to possess the whole of the continent which Providence has given us for the development of the great experiment of liberty and federated self-government entrusted to us."

26. James Russell Lowell uses a fictitious New England farmer and abolitionist named Hosea Biglow to express his opposition to the Mexican War, 1845:

"Per the barthrights of our race;
They jest want this Californy
So's to lug new slave-states in
To abuse ye, an' to scorn ye,
An' to plunder ye like sin."

27. Elizabeth Cady Stanton opens the Declaration of Sentiments issued by the women's rights convention held at Seneca Falls, New York, 1848. Note that her wording is modeled after the Declaration of Independence:

"We hold these truths to be self-evident: that all men and women are created equal; that they are endowed by their Creator with certain inalienable rights; that among these are life, liberty, and the pursuit of happiness; that to secure these rights governments are instituted, deriving their just powers from the consent of the governed."

28. **A nativist uses a political handbill to express his support for the Know-Nothing Party's opposition to Irish and German immigrants, 1854:**

    "The Irish are making our elections scenes of violence and fraud...Americans! Shall we be ruled by Irish and Germans?

29. **The platform of the Know-Nothing Party expresses the nativist opposition to immigrants and immigration, 1856:**

    "Americans must rule America; and to this end, native-born citizens should be elected for all state, federal, or municipal offices of government employment, in preference to naturalized citizens."

30. **John Brown reflecting on his future as he watched the town of Osawatomie, Kansas, burn, 1856:**

    "I have only a short time to live-only one death to die, and I will die fighting for the cause. There will be no more peace in this land until slavery is done for."

31. **Chief Justice Roger Taney speaking for the Supreme Court ruling in the Dred Scott case that African Americans are not citizens, 1857:**

    "The descendants of Africans who were imported into this country, and sold as slaves...are not included, and were not intended to be included, under the word 'citizens' in the Constitution, and can therefore claim none of the rights and privileges which that instrument provides for and secures to citizens of the United States."

32. **Stephen A. Douglas defines popular sovereignty during the Lincoln-Douglas debates, 1858:**

    "The great principle is the right of every community to judge and decide for itself whether a thing is right or wrong... It is no answer to this argument to say that slavery is an evil, and hence should not be tolerated. You must allow the people to decide for themselves whether it is a good or an evil."

33. John Brown dedicates his life to the abolitionist cause, 1859:

"Now, if it is deemed necessary that I should forfeit my life, for the furtherance of the ends of justice, and mingle my blood further with the blood of my children and with the blood of millions in this slave country whose rights are disregarded by wicked, cruel, and unjust enactments, I say, let it be done!"

34. General William T. Sherman explains the scorched-earth strategy he used during his famous "March to the Sea," 1864:

"We are not only fighting hostile armies, but a hostile people... We cannot change the hearts of those people... but we can make war so terrible...and make them so sick of war that generations would pass away before they would again appeal to it... If we can march a well-appointed army right through (the enemy's) territory, it is a demonstration to the world, foreign and domestic, that we have a power which (the enemy) cannot resist. This may not be war, but rather statesmanship."

35. The Thirteenth Amendment abolishes slavery, thus superseding the Emancipation Proclamation, 1865:

"Neither slavery nor involuntary servitude, except as a punishment for crime whereof the party shall have been duly convicted, shall exist within the United States, or any place subject to their jurisdiction."

36. A Chinese migrant to Oregon poignantly conveys the disruptions, losses, and hardships that accompanied his life in a strange new land, 1860s:

"It has been several autumns now since your dull husband left you for a far remote alien land... Because of our destitution I went out, trying to make a living. Who could know that Fate is always opposite to a man's design? Because I panned no gold, I am detained in this secluded corner of a strange land."

KEY QUOTES

37. Oliver Wendell Holmes, Jr. expresses a view closely related to Pragmatism, 1881:

"The life of the law has not been logic; it has been experience... The law embodies the story of a nation's development through many centuries, and it cannot be dealt with as if it contained only the axioms and corollaries of a book of mathematics."

38. Helen Hunt Jackson expresses her outrage toward the systematic mistreatment of Native Americans in *A Century of Dishonor*, 1881. It is important to remember that *A Century of Dishonor* helped mobilize public support for the Dawes Severalty Act.

"The tale of the wrongs, the oppressions, the murders of the Pacific-slope Indians in the last thirty years would be a volume by itself, and is too monstrous to be believed."

39. Andrew Carnegie explains his belief in the Gospel of Wealth, that the rich have a responsibility to serve society by using their wealth to support worthy causes, 1889:

"This, then, is held to be the duty of the man of wealth... to consider all surplus revenues which come to him simply as trust funds, which he is called upon to administer and strictly bound as a matter of duty to administer in the manner which, in his judgment, is best calculated to produce the most beneficial results for the community— the man of wealth thus becoming the mere agent and trustee for his poorer brethen."

40. The Sherman Antitrust Act prohibits business activities that are deemed to be anticompetitive, 1890. However, the courts used the act to limit the power of labor unions.

"Every contract, combination in form of trust or otherwise, or conspiracy, in restraint of trade or commerce in any territory of the United States...is hereby declared illegal."

KEY QUOTES

41. Frederick Jackson Turner states the central point of his famous thesis, that the frontier experience played a key role in shaping American democracy, 1893:

"From the beginning of the settlement of America, the frontier regions have exercised a steady influence toward democracy... American democracy is fundamentally the outcome of the experience of the American people in dealing with the West..."

42. Booker T. Washington uses his Atlanta Compromise speech to describe his accommodationist view of the relationship between African Americans and Whites, 1895:

"In all things that are purely social we can be as separate as the fingers, yet one as the hand in all things essential to material progress... The wisest among my race understand that the agitation of questions of racial equality is the extremist folly, and that progress in the enjoyment of all the privileges that will come to use must be the result of severe and constant struggle rather than of artificial forcing."

43. Senator Henry Cabot Lodge condemning President Cleveland's isolationist policies and urging the United States to adopt an expansionist foreign policy, 1895:

"If the Democratic Party has had one cardinal principle beyond all others, it has been that of pushing forward the boundaries of the United States. Under this administration, this great principle has been utterly abandoned... Mr. Cleveland has labored to overthrow American interests and American control in Hawaii. Andrew Jackson fought for Florida but Mr. Cleveland is eager to abandon Samoa."

44. William Jennings Bryan advocates Free Silver in his famous "Cross of Gold" speech, 1896:

"You shall not crucify mankind upon a cross of gold."

45. Winston Churchill uses racial fears to argue that the United States should not intervene in Cuba, 1896:

"Two-fifths of the insurgents in the field are negroes. If these men win, they would demand a predominant share in the government of the country. In the revolution, not only the principal leaders are colored men, but at least eight-tenths of their supporters."

46. John D. Rockefeller Jr. defends monopoly capitalism in this famous quote from an address to students at Brown University given in the late 1890s:

"The growth of a large business corporation is merely survival of the fittest... The American Beauty rose can be produced in the splendor and fragrance which bring cheer to its beholder only by sacrificing the early buds which grow up around it. This is not an evil tendency in business. It is merely the working out of a law of nature an a law of God."

47. Senator Albert J. Beveridge expressing his support for U.S. imperialism, 1900:

"God has not been preparing the English-speaking and Teutonic people for a thousand years for nothing but vain and idle self-contemplation and self-admiration. No! He has made us the Master organizers of the world to establish system where chaos reigns. He has given us the spirit of progress to overwhelm the forces of reaction throughout the earth...And of all our race He has marked the American people as His chosen nation to finally lead in the regeneration of the world."

KEY QUOTES

48. George Washington Plunkitt defends the spoils system, 1905:

"When the people elected Tammany, they knew just what they were doin'. We didn't put up any false pretenses. We didn't go in for humbug civil service and all that rot. We stood as we have always stood, for rewardin' the men that won the victory... When we go in, we fire every anti-Tammany man from office that can be fired under the law."

49. International Harvester uses these lines in a company brochure to teach its workers the principles of Taylorism, early 1900s:

"I hear the whistle. I must hurry.
It is time to go into the shop.
I change my clothes and get ready to work.
The starting whistle blows."

50. Upton Sinclair describes the unsanitary conditions in a Chicago meatpacking plant in his novel *The Jungle*, 1906. Sinclair's vivid description galvanized public support for the Meat Inspection Act and the Pure Food and Drug Act.

"There would be meat that had tumbled out on the floor, in the dirt and sawdust, where the workers had trapped and spit uncounted billions of consumption [tuberculosis] germs. There would be meat stored in great piles in rooms; and thousands of rats would race about on it... This is no fairy story and no joke; the meat will be shoveled into carts and the man who did the shoveling will not trouble to lift out a rat even when he saw one."

51. William Graham Sumner argues that Social Darwinism is a necessary part of nature and social order, 1914:

"Competition, therefore, is a law of nature...Let it be understood that we cannot go outside of this alternative: liberty, inequality, survival of the fittest; not-liberty, equality, survival of the unfittest. The former carries society forward and favors all its best members; the latter carries society downwards and favors all its worst members."

52. Lyrics from a popular song became a popular slogan used to promote buying on an installment plan, 1931:

"A dollar down and a dollar a week"

53. Lyricist E.Y. "Yip" Hartburg expresses the despair that gripped America during the worst years of the Great Depression, 1932:

"Once I built a railroad, made it run,
Made it race against time.
Once I built a railroad, now it's done
Brother, can you spare a dime?"

54. Lyrics from the Broadway play *"42nd Street"* attempt to provide an upbeat contrast to the Great Depression then gripping the country, 1933:

"We're in the money,
We're in the money...
We never see a headline
'Bout breadline, today,
And when we see the landlord,
We can look that guy right in the eye.
We're in the money!"

KEY QUOTES

55. FDR calls for an international "quarantine of the aggressor nations" as an alternative to the political climate of neutrality and non-intervention prevalent in America, 1937:

"It seems to be unfortunately true that the epidemic of world lawlessness is spreading. When an epidemic of physical disease starts to spread, the community approves and joins in a quarantine of the patients in order to protect the health of the community against the spread of the disease."

56. FDR uses a Fireside Chat to explain the urgency of providing military aid to Great Britain, 1940:

"We must be the great arsenal of democracy. For us this is an emergency as serious as war itself. We must apply ourselves to our task with the same resolution, the same sense of urgency, the same spirit of patriotism and sacrifice as we would show were we at war."

57. Winston Churchill warns America that the Soviet Union is gaining control over Eastern Europe, 1946:

"From Stettin in the Baltic to Trieste in the Adriatic an iron curtain has descended across the Continent."

58. President Truman announces the Truman Doctrine committing America to defending the Free World, 1947:

"It must be the policy of the United States to support free peoples who are resisting attempted subjugation by armed minorities or by outside pressure."

59. Secretary of State John Marshall announces the policy of economic aid to Europe known as the Marshall Plan, 1948:

"Our policy is directed not against any country or doctrine, but against hunger, poverty, desperation, and chaos. Its purpose should be the revival of a working economy in the world so as to permit the emergence of political and social conditions in which free institutions can exist... Any government that is willing to assist in the task of recovery will find full cooperation, I am sure, on the part of the United States government."

60. Senator Joseph McCarthy launches an anti-communist campaign known as McCarthyism, 1950:

"This is the time of the Cold War... The reason why we find ourselves in a position of impotency is not because our only powerful potential enemy has sent men to invade our shores, but rather because of the traitorous actions of those who have been treated so well by this nation. It has not been the less fortunate or members of minority groups who have been selling this nation out, but rather those who have had all the benefits that the wealthiest nation on earth has had to offer."

61. President Eisenhower explains what became known as the Domino Theory to justify American support for South Vietnam, 1954:

"If Indo-China were to fall and if its fall led to the loss of all of Southeast Asia, then the United States might eventually be forced back to Hawaii, as it was before the Second World War.

KEY QUOTES

62. **Chief Justice Earl Warren speaks for a unanimous Supreme Court in *Brown v. Board of Education*, 1954. Warren believed that the Equal Protection Clause of the Fourteenth Amendment gave the Court the necessary power to reverse the "separate but equal" doctrine established in *Plessy v. Ferguson*.**

"Does segregation of children in public schools solely on the basis of race, even though the physical facilities and other tangible factors may be equal, deprive children of the minority group of equal educational opportunities? We believe that it does... We conclude that in the field of public education, the doctrine of separate but equal has no place. Separate educational facilities are inherently unequal. Therefore, we hold that the plantiff's and others similarly situated for whom the actions have been brought are, by reason of the segregation complained of, deprived of the equal protection of the laws guaranteed by the Fourteenth Amendment."

63. **President Eisenhower explains why he must send troops to Little Rock, Arkansas, to enforce desegregation orders, 1957:**

"The very basis of our individual rights and freedoms rests upon the certainty that the President and the Executive Branch of Government will support and insure the carrying out of the decisions of the federal courts, even when necessary, with all the means at the President's command."

64. **Rachel Carson warns about the deleterious effects of pesticides in her landmark book *Silent Spring*, 1962:**

"The history of life on earth has been a history of interaction between living things and their surroundings. To a large extent, the physical form and the habits of the earth's vegetation and its animal life have been molded by the environment... The most alarming of all man's assaults upon the environment is the contamination of air, earth, rivers, and sea with dangerous and even lethal materials."

65. Martin Luther King Jr. explains the need for demonstrations in Birmingham in his famous Letter from Birmingham Jail, 1963:

"We know through painful experience that freedom is never voluntarily given by the oppressor; it must be demanded by the oppressed."

66. Dr. King explains why nonviolent civil disobedience is the most effective civil rights strategy, 1958-1968:

"During the days of the Montgomery bus boycott, I came to see the power of nonviolence more and more. As I lived through the actual experience of protest, nonviolence became more than a useful method, it became a way of life."

"An individual who breaks a law that conscience tells him is unjust, and who willingly accepts the penalty of imprisonment in order to arouse the conscience of the community over its injustice, is in reality expressing the highest respect for the law."

"The problem with hatred and violence is that they intensify the fears of the white majority, and leave them less ashamed of their prejudices toward Negroes. In the guilt and confusion confronting our society, violence only adds to the chaos. It deepens the brutality of the oppressor and increases the bitterness of the oppressed. Violence is the antithesis of creativity and wholeness. It destroys community and makes brotherhood impossible."

67. Betty Friedan challenges the cult of domesticity in her groundbreaking book, *The Feminist Mystique*, 1963:

"Each suburban wife struggled with it alone. As she made the beds, shopped for groceries, matched slipcover material, ate peanut butter sandwiches with her children, chauffered Cub Scouts and Brownies, lay beside her husband at night—she was afraid to ask even of herself the silent question—'Is this all?'"

KEY QUOTES

68. Malcolm X declares that Black militancy will soon replace Dr. King's nonviolent methods, 1964:

"When I say fight for independence right here, I don't mean any nonviolent fight, or turn-the-other cheek fight. Those days are gone, those days are over."

69. LBJ explaining that the media plays a major role in shaping public opinion and has an obligation to cover events responsibly, 1968:

"The security, the success of our country...rests squarely upon the media, which disseminates the truth on which the decisions of democracy are made. You are the keepers of a trust and you must be just. You must guard and you must defend your media...against the works of divisiveness, against bigotry, against the corrupting evils of partisanship in any guise."

70. President Ford telling the American people that the Watergate crisis is over and that he is the nation's new president, 1974:

"My fellow Americans, our long national nightmare is over... Our Constitution works; our great Republic is a government of laws and not of men. Here the people rule".

—PART 4—
KEY
LISTS

KEY FEMALE LEADERS

IN THE COLONIAL ERA

1. ANNE HUTCHINSON (1594–1643)
   - Banished from Massachusetts Bay
   - Challenged the clergy's ability to interpret the Bible

2. ABIGAIL ADAMS (1744–1818)
   - Wrote a letter to her husband, John Adams, urging him to "Remember the Ladies"
   - Urged her husband to extend the benefits and rights of his republican ideas to colonial women

IN THE FIGHT AGAINST SLAVERY

3. SARAH MOORE GRIMKÉ (1792–1873)
   - Supported both abolition and women's rights

4. SOJOURNER TRUTH (1797–1883)
   - Former slave and leading abolitionist and women's rights activist

5. HARRIET BEECHER STOWE (1811–1896)
   - Author of *Uncle Tom's Cabin*
   - Book was second only to the Bible in sales
   - Book intensified Northern opposition to slavery

IN THE FIGHT FOR AFRICAN AMERICAN CIVIL RIGHTS

6. IDA B. WELLS-BARNETT (1862–1931)
   - African American civil rights activist who opposed lynching

IN THE FIGHT FOR WOMEN'S SUFFRAGE

7. ELIZABETH CADY STANTON (1815–1902)
   - Organized the Seneca Falls Convention to work for women's rights
   - Wrote the "Declaration of Sentiments" advocating suffrage based upon the principles of equality for both men and women

8. LUCRETIA MOTT (1793–1880)
   - Worked with Elizabeth Cady Stanton at the Seneca Falls Convention
   - Leading women's rights activist

KEY LISTS

9. **SUSAN B. ANTHONY (1820-1906)**
   - Prominent civil rights leader who supported women's suffrage

10. **CARRIE CHAPMAN CATT (1859-1947)**
    - Her "winning plan" helped lead to the enactment of the Nineteenth Amendment giving women the right to vote

11. **ALICE PAUL (1885-1977)**
    - Militant suffragist who worked for the Nineteenth Amendment giving women the right to vote

IN 19TH CENTURY MOVEMENTS TO REFORM AMERICAN SOCIETY

12. **EMMA WILLARD (1787-1870)**
    - Leading advocate of women's education
    - Founded the first school in America to offer higher education for women

13. **DOROTHEA DIX (1802-1887)**
    - Reformer who worked to improve the treatment of the mentally ill
    - Dix was NOT a leading feminist

14. **CATHERINE BEECHER (1800-1878)**
    - Supported the cult of domesticity
    - Argued that a woman's moral qualities should influence her husband and sons to act more virtuously

15. **CLARA BARTON (1821-1912)**
    - Founded the American Red Cross

16. **JANE ADDAMS (1860-1935)**
    - Leader of the settlement house movement
    - Founded Hull House
    - Did NOT work to promote women's rights

17. **MARY ELLEN LEASE (1850-1933)**
    - Militant Populist leader who advised Midwestern farmers to "Raise less corn and more hell."

18. **HELEN HUNT JACKSON (1830-1885)**
    - Documented the government's mistreatment of Native Americans in her book *A Century of Dishonor*
    - *A Century of Dishonor* played a key role in persuading Congress to pass the Dawes Act

KEY LISTS

IN 20TH CENTURY MOVEMENTS TO REFORM AMERICAN SOCIETY

19. **CARRIE NATION (1846-1911)**
    - Outspoken leader in the Women's Christian Temperance Union
    - Best known for smashing bars with her trademark hatchet

20. **IDA TARBELL (1857-1944)**
    - Muckraker and investigative reporter
    - Exposed the questionable business practices of the Standard Oil Company

21. **MARGARET SANGER (1879-1966)**
    - Outspoken supporter of birth control

22. **ELEANOR ROOSEVELT (1884-1962)**
    - Champion of equal rights and the poor during the New Deal era
    - Resigned from the Daughters of the American Revolution to protest their refusal to allow African American singer Marion Anderson to perform at Constitution Hall

23. **RACHEL CARSON (1907-1964)**
    - Wrote *Silent Spring* to warn about the damaging effects of chemical pesticides
    - *Silent Spring* helped launch the national environmental movement

IN THE MODERN FEMINIST MOVEMENT

24. **BETTY FRIEDAN (1921-2006)**
    - Author of *The Feminist Mystique*, which asked "Is this all?"
    - First president of the National Organization for Women (NOW)
    - Criticized traditional gender roles

25. **GLORIA STEINEM (1934-present)**
    - Feminist leader and co-founder of *Ms. Magazine*

IN MODERN POLITICS

26. **PHYLLIS SCHLAFLY (1924-present)**
    - Led a successful campaign to block the passage of the Equal Rights Amendment

27. **GERALDINE FERRARO (1935-2011)**
    - First female vice-presidential candidate of a major political party

IN LITERATURE AND CULTURE

28. **ANNE BRADSTREET (1612-1672)**
    - First published female poet and writer in the British North American colonies

29. **PHYLLIS WHEATLEY (1753-1784)**
    - First published African American woman in the British North American colonies

30. **BILLIE HOLLIDAY (1915-1959)**
    - Famous jazz singer in the 1930s and 1940s

31. **GEORGIA O'KEEFFE (1887-1986)**
    - Famous Modernist artist whose work portrayed scenes in the American Southwest

KEY MALE LEADERS

IN THE FIGHT AGAINST SLAVERY

1. JOHN BROWN (1800-1859)
- Led a raid on Harper's Ferry that helped convince the South that the North wanted to instigate a slave rebellion
- Inspired other abolitionists by declaring, "I have only a short time to live—only one death to die, and I will die fighting for a cause"

2. WILLIAM LLOYD GARRISON (1805-1879)
- Founded *The Liberator*, a newspaper dedicated to championing the abolition of slavery
- Called for the immediate and unconditional abolition of slavery

3. FREDERICK DOUGLASS (1818-1895)
- Former slave who became the leading African American abolitionist

IN THE STRUGGLE FOR CIVIL RIGHTS

4. BOOKER T. WASHINGTON (1856-1915)
- Advocated African American self-help and vocational education
- Opposed political agitation

5. W.E.B. Du BOIS (1868-1963)
- Opposed Booker T. Washington's accommodationist program
- Favored "unceasing agitation" to gain full political, economic, and social equality
- Urged the "talented tenth" to spearhead reform for equality
- Approved the NAACP's strategy of using the courts to strike down Jim Crow segregation laws

6. MARCUS GARVEY (1887-1940)
- Emphasized the importance of Black pride and Black nationalism
- Committed to the idea that Black Americans should return to Africa
- Led the Universal Negro Improvement Association

7. CLAUDE McKAY (1889-1945)
- Leading Harlem Renaissance author
- Advocated the New Negro, calling for African Americans to adopt a new sense of racial pride

8. MALCOLM X (1925-1965)
   - Key Black Muslim leader
   - Opposed Dr. King's strategy of nonviolent civil disobedience
   - Believed in Black separatism

9. DR. MARTIN LUTHER KING JR. (1929-1968)
   - Advocated a strategy of nonviolent civil disobedience
   - Influenced by the writings of Henry David Thoreau and Gandhi
   - Achieved national prominence during the Montgomery Bus Boycott
   - Led the Southern Christian Leadership Conference (SCLC)

10. STOKELY CARMICHAEL (1941-1998)
   - Led the Student Nonviolent Coordinating Committee (SNCC)
   - Outspoken proponent of Black Power

IN THE STRUGGLE FOR LABOR RIGHTS

11. TERENCE POWDERLY (1849-1924)
   - Led the Knights of Labor
   - Advocated an open-membership policy welcoming both skilled and unskilled workers into "one big union"

12. SAMUEL GOMPERS (1850-1924)
   - Led the American Federation of Labor (AFL)
   - Advocated an alliance of skilled workers organized into craft unions
   - Focused on "bread and butter" unionism by concentrating on demands for higher wages, shorter hours, and better working conditions

13. EUGENE DEBS (1855-1926)
   - Believed that the capitalist system was flawed
   - Advocated government control over key industries and natural resources

14. JOHN L. LEWIS (1880-1969)
   - Led the Congress of Industrial Organizations (CIO)
   - Organized unskilled and semiskilled factory workers in basic manufacturing industries such as steel and automobiles

15. CEASAR CHAVEZ (1927-1993)
   - Led the United Farm Workers (UFW)
   - Led a historic strike by California grape pickers

IN THE STRUGGLE TO REFORM AMERICAN SOCIETY

16. **HORACE MANN (1796-1859)**
    - Promoted public education

17. **JACOB RIIS (1849-1914)**
    - Remembered as a journalist and photographer who publicized the deplorable conditions endured by poor urban residents in the early 20th century

18. **JOHN DEWEY (1859-1952)**
    - Progressive educator who believed that children learn by doing

19. **RALPH NADER (1934-present)**
    - Champion of consumer rights
    - Publicized the dangers of nuclear waste

IN THE STRUGGLE TO CONTAIN COMMUNISM

20. **WINSTON CHURCHILL (1874-1965)**
    - A member of the "Big Three" along with FDR and Stalin in the Second World War
    - Delivered the "Iron Curtain" speech to warn America that the Soviet Union was creating a sphere of influence in Eastern Europe

21. **GEORGE KENNAN (1904-2005)**
    - Remembered as the "Father of Containment"
    - Argued that the United States should adopt a policy of blocking the expansion of Soviet influence

22. **GEORGE MARSHALL (1880-1959)**
    - Served as Secretary of State under President Truman
    - Supported the Marshall Plan to promote Europe's economic recovery in the years following the Second World War

23. **JOHN FOSTER DULLES (1888-1959)**
    - Served as Secretary of State under President Eisenhower
    - Advocated the Cold War policies of brinksmanship and massive retaliation

IN THE WORLD OF POLITICS

24. ALEXANDER HAMILTON (1755-1804)
- Served as America's first Secretary of Treasury
- Advocated a loose interpretation of the Constitution
- Used the "necessary and proper clause" to justify the constitutionality of the National Bank
- Favored a national debt in order to link the interests of wealthy Americans with the federal government
- Supported eastern merchants, manufacturing, and an aristocracy of talent

25. JOHN MARSHALL (1755-1835)
- Served as Chief Justice of the Supreme Court from 1801 to 1835
- Established the principle of judicial review in *Marbury v. Madison*
- Judicial rulings placed federal law above state laws by supporting the sanctity of contracts and Congressional control over interstate commerce

26. JOHN C. CALHOUN (1782-1850)
- Began his political career as a "War Hawk" who supported territorial expansion as a goal during the War of 1812
- Advocated states' rights and the doctrine of nullification
- Opposed high protective tariffs

27. HENRY CLAY (1777-1852)
- Began his political career as a "War Hawk" who supported territorial expansion as a goal during the War of 1812
- Championed an "American System" that supports a national bank and high protective tariffs that would fund a program of internal improvements that included canals and turnpikes

28. STEPHEN A. DOUGLAS (1813-1861)
- Advocated popular sovereignty to determine the status of slavery in the western territories

29. WILLIAM M. "BOSS" TWEED (1823-1878)
- Led the corrupt Tammany Hall political machine in New York City
- Satirized in Thomas Nast political cartoons as a rotund, cigar smoking politician with a money bag for a head

KEY LISTS

30. **WILLIAM JENNINGS BRYAN (1860-1925)**
    - Opposed the gold standard and strongly supported free silver
    - Nominated for president in 1896 by the Democrats on a platform that included many Populist goals
    - Drew strong support from farmers in Kansas and other Midwestern states

31. **HENRY CABOT LODGE (1850-1924)**
    - Served as a U.S. Senator from Massachusetts
    - Supported overseas territorial expansion
    - Opposed U.S. participation in the League of Nations

32. **JOSEPH McCARTHY (1908-1957)**
    - Led a campaign against alleged Communists and Communist sympathizers
    - Accused public officials of disloyalty without sufficient evidence
    - Lost influence following the televised Army-McCarthy hearings

33. **WILLIAM FULBRIGHT (1905-1995)**
    - Leading Senate critic of the Vietnam War
    - Wrote *The Arrogance of Power*

34. **GEORGE WALLACE (1919-1998)**
    - Championed segregation while serving as governor of Alabama
    - Formed and led the American Independent Party
    - Appealed to middle and working class citizens upset by antiwar demonstrations and urban riots

IN THE WORLD OF RELIGION

35. **JOHN WINTHROP (1587-1649)**
    - Led the Massachusetts Bay Colony
    - Urged Puritans to build a model Christian community that would serve as a "City Upon a Hill."

36. **ROGER WILLIAMS (1603-1683)**
    - Banished from Massachusetts Bay for his unorthodox views
    - Supported freedom of religion and the separation of church and state
    - Defended liberty of conscience on the grounds that the state was an improper and ineffectual agency in matters of the spirit
    - Founded the Rhode Island colony

37. **JONATHAN EDWARDS (1703-1758)**
   - Renowned as a Christian preacher and theologian during the First Great Awakening
   - Remembered for his famous sermon "Sinners in the Hands of an Angry God"

38. **GEORGE WHITEFIELD (1714-1770)**
   - Renowned for his emotional sermons during the First Great Awakening

39. **CHARLES GRANDISON FINNEY (1792-1875)**
   - Renowned for emotional Second Great Awakening sermons delivered in New York state's "burned over district"

40. **BRIGHAM YOUNG (1801-1877)**
   - Led the Mormon Trek to Utah
   - Supported polygamy
   - Opposed women's suffrage

IN THE WORLD OF INDUSTRY AND BUSINESS

41. **ELI WHITNEY (1765-1825)**
   - Invented the cotton gin
   - Helped develop the use of interchangeable parts for the manufacture of firearms

42. **ANDREW CARNEGIE (1835-1919)**
   - Used vertical integration to gain control of the steel industry
   - Argued in the Gospel of Wealth that the rich have a duty to use their wealth to serve society.

43. **HENRY FORD (1863-1947)**
   - Applied the principles of the moving assembly line to the manufacture of automobiles
   - Pioneered the forty-hour work week and the five-dollar workday
   - Supported isolationism during the 1930s

44. **FREDERICK TAYLOR (1856-1915)**
   - Pioneered a system of scientific management designed to eliminate wasted motion

45. **WILLIAM RANDOLPH HEARST (1863-1951)**
   - Combative newspaper publisher who used "yellow journalism" to create public support for the Spanish-American War

KEY LISTS

IN THE WORLD OF ART, LITERATURE AND THOUGHT

46. UPTON SINCLAIR (1878-1968)
- Wrote the muckraking novel *The Jungle*
- Exposed appalling conditions in Chicago meatpacking plants
- Helped arouse public support for the Meat Inspection Act and the Pure Food and Drug Act

47. ALFRED MAHAN (1840-1914)
- Wrote *The Influence of Sea Power upon History*
- Urged America to build the Panama Canal and construct a powerful navy

48. FREDERICK JACKSON TURNER (1861-1932)
- Wrote "The Significance of the Frontier in American History"
- Argued that the frontier experience played a key role in the development of American individualism and democratic institutions

49. JACKSON POLLOCK (1912-1956)
- Leading figure in the artistic movement known as Abstract Expressionism

50. ANDY WARHOL (1928-1987)
- Leading figure in the artistic movement known as Pop Art
- Best known for his Pop Art paintings of Campbell's Soup cans and celebrities such as Elvis Presley and Marilyn Monroe

KEY LISTS

KEY PRESIDENTS

1. GEORGE WASHINGTON (1789-1797)
- Understood that the Continental Army was an important symbol of Republicanism
- Published a Farewell Address warning against forming permanent alliances with foreign powers
- Opponents of the League of Nations and isolationists used the Farewell Address to buttress their opposition to foreign involvement

2. JOHN ADAMS (1797-1801)
- Approved the Alien and Sedition Acts

3. THOMAS JEFFERSON (1801-1809)
- Believed that the farmer is the backbone of American society; freedom of speech is essential in a republic; the president should practice republican simplicity; and that the government is best that governs least
- Favored a strict constructionist view of the Constitution
- Opposed the National Bank
- Praised the election of 1800 as a "revolution" because it marked a peaceful transfer of power
- Accepted the Louisiana Purchase despite his constitutional objections
- Advocated land sales to promote small farmers
- Believed that America should be governed by an aristocracy of talent

4. JAMES MADISON (1809-1817)
- Argued that an expanding republic with vast territory would curb factionalism and tyranny

5. JAMES MONROE (1817-1825)
- President during the Era of Good Feelings
- Issued a unilateral declaration of principles later known as the Monroe Doctrine
- Warned European nations against further colonial ventures in the Western Hemisphere
- Approved the Adams-Onis Treaty defining the western border of the Louisiana Territory and ceding Florida to the United States

6. JOHN QUINCY ADAMS (1825-1829)
- Elected by a controversial vote in the House of Representatives

KEY LISTS

7. ANDREW JACKSON (1829-1837)
- Status as a wealthy planter contradicted his image as a hero of the common man
- Reputation as a war hero in the War of 1812 helped him win the election of 1828
- Opposed the Bank of the United States because it favored wealthy elites
- Supported the Indian Removal Act
- Opposed Calhoun's doctrine of nullification
- Resisted the annexation of Texas because of fears it would ignite the controversy over slavery
- Supported the spoils system as a method of appointing supporters to government positions
- Vetoed the Mayville Road bill as an of strict constructionism
- Sectional disputes over tariffs dominated much of his presidency

8. WILLIAM HENRY HARRISON (1841)
- Promoted as a champion of the common man in the "log cabin and hard cider" campaign

9. JAMES K. POLK (1845-1849)
- Advocated territorial expansion from ocean to ocean
- Campaigned on the slogan "Fifty Four-Fourty' or Fight" to acquire all of the Oregon Territory

10. ABRAHAM LINCOLN (1861-1865)
- Did NOT participate in the negotiations over the Compromise of 1850
- Used the Dred Scott decision to question Stephen A. Douglas in the Lincoln-Douglas debates
- Elected President without carrying a single Southern state
- Suspended habeas corpus during the Civil War
- Issued the Emancipation Proclamation following the Union victory at Antietam
- Proposed a lenient Ten Percent Plan to quickly restore the Union

11. ANDREW JOHNSON (1865-1869)
- Impeached because he opposed Radical Reconstruction

12. THEODORE ROOSEVELT (1901–1909)
- Supported the conservation of natural resources and wildlife
- Built the Panama Canal
- Issued the Roosevelt Corollary to the Monroe Doctrine asserting America's right to intervene in the affairs of Central American and Caribbean nations
- Promoted a Square Deal for labor by using arbitration to settle the Anthracite Coal Strike of 1902
- Did NOT deal with insider trading on Wall Street or ask Congress to consider a constitutional amendment granting women the right to vote
- Used the Gentleman's Agreement to block Japanese immigration to the United States
- Ran as the Progressive or "Bull Moose" candidate for President in the 1912 presidential election

13. WILLIAM HOWARD TAFT (1909–1913)
- Used Dollar Diplomacy to promote American economic interests in Central America and the Caribbean

14. WOODROW WILSON (1913–1921)
- Issued the Fourteen Points calling for open diplomacy, freedom of the seas, self-determination, and a League of Nations; did NOT call for an international monetary fund
- Advocated using anti-trust laws to break up big business trusts and monopolies

15. WARREN G. HARDING (1921–1923)
- Tarnished by the Teapot Dome scandal

16. CALVIN COOLIDGE (1923–1929)
- Followed policies that favored big business

17. HERBERT HOOVER (1929–1933)
- Opposed federal relief programs to help the poor
- Established the Reconstruction Finance Corporation to help banks

KEY LISTS

18. FRANKLIN D. ROOSEVELT (1933-1945)
- Championed the New Deal to provide relief, recovery, and reform
- Used deficit spending to finance public works programs
- Sought to restructure and reform American capitalism rather than promote socialism
- Elected by a New Coalition that included African Americans, ethnic minorities, union members, and White Southerners
- Used the Lend-Lease program to help Great Britain and the Soviet Union resist Nazi Germany

19. HARRY S. TRUMAN (1945-1953)
- Justified using the atomic bomb by saying it would save the lives of American soldiers; decision was NOT influenced by public opinion
- Supported a Fair Deal to continue New Deal reforms; did NOT nationalize American industry
- Considered the Red Army to be the Soviet Union's greatest strength
- Issued the Truman Doctrine to contain the spread of Soviet influence
- Desegregated the armed forces prior to the Korean War
- Support for civil rights triggered the formation of the Dixiecrat Party
- Recalled MacArthur for insubordination

20. DWIGHT D. EISENHOWER (1953-1961)
- Enforced the Supreme Court's decision on desegregation by sending troops to Little Rock, Arkansas
- Criticized for not directly confronting Senator McCarthy
- Sponsored the Interstate Highway System
- Did NOT actively support civil rights legislation

21. JOHN F. KENNEDY (1961-1963)
- Idealized as the leader of "Camelot"
- Approved the Bay of Pigs invasion of Cuba
- Responded to the Cuban Missile Crisis by ordering a naval quarantine of Cuba
- Assassination created public support for the Civil Rights Act of 1964

KEY LISTS

22. LYNDON B. JOHNSON (1963-1969)

- Enacted Great Society programs to use education and job training to break the cycle of poverty
- Passed the Equal Opportunity Act, the Civil Rights Act of 1964, and the Voting Rights Act of 1965
- Funded the arts
- Used the Tonkin Gulf Resolution to escalate the Vietnam War
- Escalating costs of the Vietnam War undermined Great Society programs

23. RICHARD M. NIXON (1969-1974)

- Called upon the "silent majority" to support his policies in Vietnam
- Used Vietnamization to withdraw American forces from Vietnam
- Ordered the invasion of Cambodia to cut North Vietnamese supply lines; triggered college protests and the Kent State shootings
- Visited China and Moscow as part of a policy of détente
- Signed a Strategic Arms Limitation treaty with the Soviet Union
- Promoted New Federalism as a way to distribute federal funds to state and local governments
- Tried to use executive privilege to justify withholding key Watergate information
- Forced to resign because of the Watergate scandal

24. GERALD FORD (1974-1977)

- Declared that "Our long national nightmare is over" following Nixon's resignation
- Pardoned Nixon and then suffered a loss of popularity
- Failed to curtail the rising rate of inflation

25. JIMMY CARTER (1977-1981)

- Made human rights the centerpiece of his foreign policy
- Popularity undermined by inflation, high interest rates, and the Iran hostage crisis
- Union membership did NOT increase during his administration
- Camp David Accords marked his greatest success
- Three Mile Island accident undermined public support for nuclear power

KEY LISTS

26. RONALD REAGAN (1981-1989)
- Implemented a series of supply-side economic programs known as Reaganomics
- Deregulated business to promote economic growth
- Supported tax cuts that led to large increases in the incomes of wealthy Americans
- Accused of being insensitive to the poor and using the "Star Wars" program to cut social spending
- Declared the Reagan Doctrine to oppose and confront the Soviet Union

27. GEORGE H. W. BUSH (1989-1993)
- Organized an international coalition to liberate Kuwait

28. BILL CLINTON (1993-2001)
- Approved the North American Free Trade Agreement (NAFTA) and the World Trade Organization (WTO)
- Impeached by the House of Representatives for perjury and obstruction of justice
- Failed to pass healthcare reform legislation
- Successfully enacted welfare reform legislation.

29. GEORGE W. BUSH (2001-2009)
- Ordered an attack on the Taliban in Afghanistan in the months immediately following the 9/11 attacks
- Used the alleged existence of Weapons of Mass Destruction as a reason to invade Iraq and overthrow Saddam Hussein

KEY LISTS

KEY PRESIDENTIAL ELECTIONS

1. **THE ELECTION OF 1800**
   - Referred to as the "Revolution of 1800" because the Federalists peacefully gave up power after losing the election to Jefferson
   - Ended the "Federalist Decade"

2. **THE ELECTION OF 1816**
   - Monroe's victory ushered in the Era of Good Feelings
   - Began a period of national unity

3. **THE ELECTION OF 1824**
   - John Quincy Adams chosen by the House of Representatives amidst charges of a "corrupt bargain"

4. **THE ELECTION OF 1828**
   - Jackson's election viewed as a victory for the common man

5. **THE ELECTION OF 1840**
   - Harrison's campaign successfully used the "log cabin and hard cider" slogan to appeal to the common-man vote

6. **THE ELECTION OF 1860**
   - Lincoln won the electoral vote but failed to carry a single Southern state
   - South Carolina and six other Southern states secede

7. **THE ELECTION OF 1876**
   - Samuel Tilden won the popular vote but lost the electoral vote to Hayes
   - The election of Hayes ended Reconstruction

8. **THE ELECTION OF 1896**
   - McKinley defeated Bryan in a victory for the gold standard
   - Began an era of Republican dominance

9. **THE ELECTION OF 1912**
   - Theodore Roosevelt formed the Bull Moose Party, splitting the Republican vote and enabling Wilson to win

KEY LISTS

10. THE ELECTION OF 1936
- African Americans switched their votes to the Democratic Party
- New Deal coalition of African Americans, labor unions, big city machines, and White Southerners won a landslide victory

11. THE ELECTION OF 1948
- Southern delegates walked out of the Democratic Convention to protest Truman's civil rights proposals
- Truman won an upset victory over Dewey

12. THE ELECTION OF 1960
- First televised debates helped JFK win a razor thin majority
- Kennedy became America's first Catholic president

13. THE ELECTION OF 1980
- Inflation and the Iran Hostage Crisis helped Reagan defeat Carter
- Reagan received strong support from the "New Right"

KEY CONSTITUTIONAL AMENDMENTS

1. **THE FIRST AMENDMENT**
   - Guarantees freedom of religion, speech, press, and the right of the public to peaceably assemble

2. **THE FOURTH AMENDMENT**
   - Forbids unreasonable searches
   - Response to the British writs of assistance

3. **THE SIXTH AMENDMENT**
   - Guaranteed an accused person the right to a speedy trial

4. **THE THIRTEENTH AMENDMENT**
   - Abolished slavery
   - Superseded the Emancipation Proclamation

5. **THE FOURTEENTH AMENDMENT**
   - Granted citizenship to former slaves
   - Invalidated the Dred Scott decision
   - Includes both a "due process clause" and an "equal protection clause"
   - The Warren Court used the equal protection clause to reverse the doctrine of separate but equal established in *Plessy v. Ferguson*

6. **THE FIFTEENTH AMENDMENT**
   - Enfranchised African American males
   - Antagonized proponents of women's suffrage

7. **THE SIXTEENTH AMENDMENT**
   - Granted Congress the power to lay and collect income taxes

8. **THE SEVENTEENTH AMENDMENT**
   - Established the direct election of U.S. Senators by the voters in each state

KEY LISTS

9. THE EIGHTEENTH AMENDMENT
- Forbade the manufacture of intoxicating liquors
- Reversed by the Twenty-First Amendment

10. NINETEENTH AMENDMENT
- Enfranchised women voters

11. THE TWENTY-FOURTH AMENDMENT
- Abolished the poll tax
- Was not passed during the Progressive era

KEY ACTS

1. **MARYLAND TOLERATION ACT (1649)**
    - Protected the religious rights of Catholic settlers in Maryland

2. **NAVIGATION ACTS (1651)**
    - Put mercantilism into practice
    - Listed colonial products that could only be shipped to England
    - Designed to subordinate the colonial economy to that of the mother country
    - Not enforced during the period of salutary neglect

3. **SUGAR ACT (1754)**
    - First law passed by Parliament to raise revenue
    - Increased the custom duty on sugar imported from the West Indies

4. **STAMP ACT (1765)**
    - Designed to raise revenue to support British troops stationed in America
    - Provoked a debate over Parliament's right to tax the American colonies
    - Repealed because colonial boycotts of English goods were hurting British merchants

5. **DECLARATORY ACT (1766)**
    - Declared that Parliament had the right to tax the colonies
    - Issued in response to the repeal of the Stamp Act

6. **COERCIVE ACTS (1774)**
    - British response to the Boston Tea Party
    - Widely known in the colonies as the Intolerable Acts
    - Designed to punish Boston and increase British control over the Massachusetts colony

7. **ALIEN AND SEDITION ACTS (1798)**
    - Designed to intimidate critics of the Adams' administration
    - Prompted Jefferson and Madison to write the Virginia and Kentucky Resolutions

KEY LISTS

8. **EMBARGO ACT OF 1807**
    - Intended to maintain American neutrality in the war between England and France
    - Harmed the U.S. economy more than the economies of either France or Britain
    - Had the unanticipated effect of promoting the growth of American manufacturing

9. **KANSAS-NEBRASKA ACT (1854)**
    - Repealed the Missouri Compromise
    - Heightened sectional tensions
    - Permitted the expansion of slavery based upon the principle of popular sovereignty
    - Led to the formation of the Republican Party
    - Led to the demise of the Whig Party

10. **HOMESTEAD ACT (1862)**
    - Encouraged the settlement of the Western frontier
    - Kept the Republican promise of "free land for free men"

11. **MORRILL LAND GRANT ACT (1862)**
    - Encouraged states to use money raised from the sale of land to fund state colleges

12. **CHINESE EXCLUSION ACT OF 1882**
    - First law to exclude a group from America because of ethnic background
    - Prohibited the immigration of Chinese to America
    - Strongly supported by working-class Americans
    - Reflected anti-immigration sentiment in California and the West Coast

13. **DAWES SEVERALTY ACT (1887)**
    - Received public support because of Helen Hunt Jackson's book *A Century of Dishonor*
    - Divided Native American tribal lands into individual plots
    - Intended to assimilate Native Americans into the mainstream of
    - American culture

14. **INTERSTATE COMMERCE ACT OF 1887**
    - Designed to stop the railroads from setting discriminatory rates
    - Set a precedent for federal regulation over interstate commerce
    - Created the first regulatory agency, the Interstate Commerce Commission (ICC)

15. **SHERMAN ANTITRUST ACT (1890)**
    - Forbade unreasonable combinations or contracts in restraint of trade
    - Used to curb labor unions
    - Served as a prohibitory act rather than a regulatory act

16. **THE PURE FOOD AND DRUG ACT (1906)**
    - Prompted by public outrage sparked by Upton Sinclair's book *The Jungle*
    - Illustrates the close connection between muckraking journalism and Progressive legislation

17. **FEDERAL RESERVE ACT OF 1913**
    - Designed to increase the stability of the U.S. financial system

18. **ESPIONAGE ACT OF 1917**
    - Criticized for threatening to take away fundamental freedoms guaranteed by the Bill of Rights

19. **NATIONAL ORIGINS ACT OF 1924**
    - Used quotas to sharply restrict the flow of immigrants from Southern and Eastern Europe

20. **NATIONAL INDUSTRIAL RECOVERY ACT OF 1933 (NRA)**
    - Allowed businesses to regulate themselves through codes of fair competition
    - Struck down by the Supreme Court

21. **AGRICULTURAL ADJUSTMENT ACT (1933)**
    - Ordered farmers to reduce the amount of land under cultivation
    - Designed to reduce the supply of farm products and thus raise crop prices

22. **NEUTRALITY ACTS (1930s)**
    - Designed to prevent the U.S. from becoming entangled in European wars

KEY LISTS

23. SECURITIES EXCHANGE ACT (1934)
- Created the Securities Exchange Commission to regulate the stock market

24. SOCIAL SECURITY ACT (1935)
- Created a federal pension system
- Part of the New Deal
- Threatened by the retirement of millions of Baby Boomers

25. WAGNER ACT (1935)
- Granted workers the right to organize and bargain collectively
- Promoted a rapid rise in labor union membership
- Also known as the National Labor Relations Act

26. LEND-LEASE ACT (1941)
- Provided military supplies to help Great Britain and the Soviet Union fight Nazi Germany

27. GI BILL (1944)
- Provided education and home or farm loans for World War II veterans
- Did NOT provide car loans

28. TAFT-HARTLEY ACT (1947)
- Designed to curb the power of labor unions
- Supported by business interests

29. McCARRAN INTERNAL SECURITY ACT (1950)
- Designed to curb Communist influence in the United States
- Required Communist organizations to register with the United States Attorney General

30. FEDERAL HIGHWAY ACT OF 1956
- Created the Interstate Highway System
- Played an important role in promoting suburban growth

31. CIVIL RIGHTS ACT OF 1964
- Used the assassination of JFK to generate pressure on Congress to pass the bill
- Outlawed discrimination in public places based upon race, color, religion, sex, or national origin

KEY LISTS

32. UNITED STATES IMMIGRATION AND NATIONALITY ACT OF 1965
- Abolished the quota system created by the National Origins Act of 1924
- Sparked a new wave of immigration from Latin America and Asia

33. WAR POWERS ACT OF 1973
- Repealed the Tonkin Gulf Resolution
- Designed to restrict the president's war-making powers

34. CIVIL LIBERTIES ACT OF 1988
- Granted a payment of $20,000 to surviving Japanese internment victims

KEY LISTS

—PART 5—
PRACTICE
TEST

1. Which of the following is NOT true of Pre-Columbian Native Americans?
   A. They developed a mathematically based calendar.
   B. They developed a strong sense of spirituality.
   C. They developed an agricultural system based upon cereal crops.
   D. They developed the water wheel.
   E. They developed a division of labor based upon gender roles.

2. "In all things purely social we can be as separate as the fingers, yet one as the hand in all things essential to mutual progress." The 1895 statement about civil rights, cited above, reflects the views of
   A. Frederick Douglass
   B. William Lloyd Garrison
   C. Booker T. Washington
   D. W.E.B. Du Bois
   E. Ida B. Wells

3. The cult of domesticity
   A. idealized women in their roles as nurturing mothers and faithful wives
   B. supported the Lowell experiment in New England factories
   C. supported the Declaration of Sentiments issued by the Seneca Falls Convention
   D. encouraged women to join utopian communities
   E. encouraged women to support the Homestead Act

4. Franklin D. Roosevelt's Good Neighbor Policy
   A. announced America's intention to join the League of Nations
   B. renounced the unilateral use of the Roosevelt Corollary
   C. permitted Great Britain to purchase war materials
   D. forgave the debts owed by Caribbean nations to the United States
   E. addressed the issues raised in the Zimmerman Note

5. Members of the Ashcan school of art are best known for their paintings of
   A. religious themes
   B. landscapes
   C. battle scenes and military commanders
   D. skyscrapers and bridges
   E. urban barrooms and tenements

6. Ronald Reagan's primary foreign policy objective was to
   A. overthrow Castro
   B. liberate Kuwait
   C. promote human rights in Africa
   D. confront and contain the Soviet Union
   E. continue the Good Neighbor Policy in Latin America

7. All of the following occurred during World War I EXCEPT:

A. the use of government propaganda to mobilize public support for the war effort

B. the public declaration of Wilson's Fourteen Points

C. the enactment of a Selective Service Act, requiring all men aged 21 to 30 to register for military service

D. the racial integration of the armed forces

E. the migration of African Americans from the rural South to cities in the North

8. *Main Street* by Sinclair Lewis offered a critique of

A. the middle-class lifestyle during the 1920s

B. the effectiveness of the New Deal during the 1930s

C. the use of women factory workers during the 1940s

D. the television programs during the 1950s

E. the baby boom generation during the 1960s

9. Détente, Vietnamization, and the Silent Majority were all associated with the presidency of

A. Lyndon B. Johnson

B. Richard Nixon

C. Gerald Ford

D. Jimmy Carter

E. Ronald Reagan

10. Religious motivation was the MOST important factor in the founding of

A. Georgia

B. North Carolina

C. Delaware

D. New York

E. Maryland

11. "The very basis of our individual rights and freedoms rests upon the certainty that the President and the Executive Branch of Government will support and insure the carrying out of the decisions of the federal courts, even, when necessary, with all the means at the President's command." Which of the following Presidents made the above statement?

A. President Jackson, explaining his decision to enforce the Supreme Court's decision in *Worcester v. Georgia*.

B. President Theodore Roosevelt, explaining his decision to send federal troops to end the Anthracite Coal Strike of 1902.

C. President Eisenhower, explaining his decision to send federal troops to Little Rock to enforce a court-ordered desegregation plan.

D. President Truman, explaining his decision to integrate the Armed Forces.

E. President Nixon, explaining his decision to use federal troops to restore order at Kent State University.

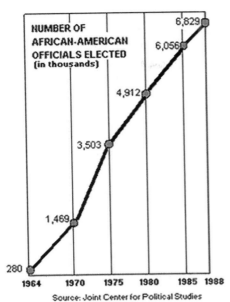

NUMBER OF
AFRICAN-AMERICAN
OFFICIALS ELECTED
(in thousands)

6,829

6,056

4,912

3,503

1,469

280

1964   1970   1975   1980   1985 1988

Source: Joint Center for Political Studies

14. Jane Addams is best known for her work
    A. opposing lynching in the South
    B. founding a college for women
    C. improving the treatment of the mentally ill
    D. promoting the settlement house movement
    E. investigating the rise of the Standard Oil Company

15. During the 1880s, nativist sentiment in California was primarily directed against
    A. Germans
    B. Poles
    C. Irish
    D. Chinese
    E. Filipinos

12. The dramatic rise in the number of African American elected officials between 1964 and 1988 (see above) can best be most directly attributed to the impact of
    A. Radical Reconstruction
    B. the Double V Campaign
    C. the Montgomery Bus Boycott
    D. the Voting Rights Act of 1965
    E. the *Regents of the University of California v. Bakke* decision

16. Which of the following best characterizes American foreign policy in the period immediately following World War I?
    A. Isolationism
    B. Containment
    C. Imperialism
    D. Dollar Diplomacy
    E. Détente

13. The Open Door was intended to support American trading opportunities in
    A. Latin America
    B. China
    C. Japan
    D. West Africa
    E. French Indochina

PRACTICE TEST

17. The Gulf of Tonkin Resolution marked an important turning point in the Vietnam War because

A. Congress rejected the Geneva Accords, and the United States replaced France as the dominant Western power in South Vietnam

B. Congress granted President Lyndon Johnson sweeping authority to escalate military action in Vietnam

C. Congress approved the domino theory as the official U.S. foreign policy in Vietnam

D. Congress endorsed President Nixon's policy of invading Cambodia

E. Congress placed restrictions on a President's ability to wage wars

18. The term "McCarthyism" refers to

A. the making of unsubstantiated public accusations of disloyalty

B. the endorsement of the middle-class lifestyle

C. the strategy of going to the brink of nuclear war without going over the edge

D. the belief that the fall of one country to Communism would inevitably lead to the fall of other nearby countries

E. the endorsement of America's goal of being the first nation to successfully send a man to the moon

19. All of the following 19th-century American authors are correctly paired with the book they are most associated with EXCEPT:

A. Herman Melville ... *Moby-Dick*

B. Walt Whitman ... *Leaves of Grass*

C. Helen Hunt Jackson ... *A Century of Dishonor*

D. Harriet Beecher Stowe ... *Uncle Tom's Cabin*

E. Ralph Waldo Emerson ... *Walden; or Life in the Woods*

20. The Double V Campaign refers to

A. Nixon's goal of achieving "peace with honor" while de-escalating American involvement in the Vietnam War

B. LBJ's goals of winning the war in Vietnam and the War on Poverty at home

C. FDR's goal of ending the Great Depression and defeating the Axis Powers

D. the African American community's goal of defeating fascism abroad and racism at home

E. the counterculture's goal of promoting peace and understanding

21. Which of the following was NOT true of the First Great Awakening?
   A. It was energized by itinerant preachers such as George Whitefield.
   B. It spread a renewed missionary spirit that led to the conversion of many African Americans.
   C. It led to an increase in the number of women in church congregations.
   D. It created divisions within both the Congregational and the Presbyterian churches.
   E. It primarily impacted merchants and townspeople in port cities such as Philadelphia and Boston.

22. The primary purpose of the Stamp Act was to
   A. support New Light colleges in New England
   B. reform the Navigation Acts.
   C. protect the infant industries in New England
   D. raise revenue for the British government
   E. increase colonial representation in Parliament

23. "But, as it is, we have the wolf by the ears, and we can neither hold him, nor safely let him go. Justice is in one scale, and self-preservation in the other." In the above quote, Thomas Jefferson uses "the wolf" as a metaphor for
   A. the French alliance
   B. the Alien and Sedition Acts
   C. the National Bank
   D. slavery
   E. states' rights

24. Which of the following states did NOT secede from the Union?
   A. Tennessee
   B. Arkansas
   C. North Carolina
   D. Louisiana
   E. Kentucky

25. Which of the following were characteristics of the Anasazi Indians?
   A. They were sedentary mound builders who lived in the Ohio River Valley.
   B. They were sedentary farmers who lived in the Southwest.
   C. They were hunters and gatherers who lived in the Eastern Woodlands.
   D. They were a tribe in the Pacific Northwest who relied upon hunting and fishing.
   E. They were a nomadic tribe best remembered for their intricate cave paintings.

26. Theodore Roosevelt's views on the importance of naval power were most strongly influenced by the writings of
   A. Alfred Thayer Mahan
   B. Henry David Thoreau
   C. Ida Tarbell
   D. Upton Sinclair
   E. Jacob Riis

PRACTICE TEST

27. Elizabeth Cady Stanton and Lucretia Mott organized a convention in Seneca Falls, New York, in 1848 to work for which of the following causes?
    A. Passage of the Wilmot Proviso.
    B. The election of Lincoln as President.
    C. The admission of California as a free state.
    D. A program of women's rights.
    E. The immediate and unconditional abolition of slavery.

28. "The great principle is the right of every community to judge and decide for itself whether a thing is right or wrong...It is no answer to this argument to say that slavery is an evil, and hence should not be tolerated. You must allow the people to decide for themselves whether it is good or evil."
    In this passage from his debates with Abraham Lincoln, Stephen A. Douglas explained the doctrine of
    A. states' rights that was embodied in the South Carolina Ordinance of Secession
    B. segregation that was later embodied in the Supreme Court's decision in *Plessy v. Ferguson*
    C. popular sovereignty that was embodied in the Kansas-Nebraska Act
    D. nullification that was used by John C. Calhoun to oppose the Tariff of Abominations
    E. imperialism that was later used by William McKinley to justify the annexation of the Philippines

29. All of the following were characteristic features of major northeastern cities in the late 19th century EXCEPT:
    A. densely populated immigrant neighborhoods
    B. big downtown department stores.
    C. influential political machines
    D. increasingly popular professional baseball teams
    E. increasing amounts of downtown land devoted to automobile parking lots

30. The Camp David Accords
    A. normalized relations between the United States and Cuba
    B. ended the Vietnam War
    C. established a new era of détente with the Soviet Union
    D. formally established diplomatic relations between the United States and the Soviet Union
    E. ended thirty years of intermittent hostility between Egypt and Israel

31. The most probable authors of statements I, II, and III:

I. "We, therefore...do declare and ordain...That the several acts... are unauthorized by the Constitution of the United States...and are null, void, and no law, nor binding upon this State, its officers or citizens."

II. "In an expanding Republic, so many different groups and viewpoints would be included in the Congress that tyranny by the majority would be impossible."

III. "A national debt if it is not excessive will be to us a national blessing, it will be a powerful cement of our union."

   A. Andrew Jackson, John Jay, and Thomas Jefferson
   B. John C. Calhoun, James Madison, and Alexander Hamilton
   C. James Madison, Thomas Jefferson, and Herbert Hoover
   D. Henry Clay, Patrick Henry, and Franklin D. Roosevelt
   E. Abraham Lincoln, James Madison, and Ronald Reagan

32. The Chisholm Trail was used by

   A. Pancho Villa to evade General Pershing
   B. Plains Indians to evade General Custer
   C. surveyors to find the best route for a Southern transcontinental railroad
   D. miners to connect silver and gold strikes in Nevada
   E. cowboys to drive cattle from ranches in Texas to railroad towns in Kansas

33. The "zoot-suit" riot was the name given to

   A. disturbances caused by hippies at the Woodstock Music Festival
   B. attacks by sailors on Mexican American youth in Los Angeles in 1943
   C. protests by members of the Anti-Imperialist League opposed to the annexation of the Philippines
   D. attacks by police on antiwar demonstrators at the 1968 Chicago Democratic convention
   E. conflict between the police and antiwar demonstrators in Washington, D.C., following the Kent State shooting in 1970

A Good Time for Reflection

Source: Library of Congress

34. Which of the following groups would be most likely to agree with the attitude toward American foreign policy expressed in this political cartoon?

A. Imperialists prior to the Spanish-American War.

B. Isolationists prior to the Second World War.

C. Cold Warriors prior to the Berlin Airlift.

D. Hawks prior to the Tonkin Gulf Resolution.

E. Bush supporters prior to the First Gulf War.

35. Which of the following nations was the first to conduct systematic maritime expeditions in the South Atlantic?

A. The Portuguese

B. The Spanish

C. The Italians

D. The English

E. The French

36. "Remember the Ladies, and be more generous and favorable to them than your ancestors. Do not put such unlimited power into the hands of the Husbands. Remember all Men would be tyrants if they could. If particular care and attention is not paid to the Ladies we are determined to foment a rebellion."

The statement above was made by

A. Anne Hutchinson, urging Jonathan Edwards to give women a greater role in the First Great Awakening

B. Anne Bradstreet, urging Patrick Henry to support the formation of a Daughters of Liberty

C. Abigail Adams, urging her husband John Adams to become an advocate for greater rights for women

D. Elizabeth Cady Stanton, urging delegates to the Seneca Falls Convention to demand equal pay or equal work

E. Sarah Grimké, urging delegates to the 1832 Democratic convention to extend the suffrage to white women

37. John Marshall is credited with advocating the doctrine of
    A. massive retaliation
    B. nullification
    C. judicial review
    D. states' rights
    E. self-determination

38. Which one of the following labor unions is INCORRECTLY matched with its core philosophy?
    A. Knights of Labor ... welcomed all workers.
    B. Industrial Workers of the World ... embraced the rhetoric of class conflict.
    C. American Federation of Labor ... concentrated on bread-and-butter issues.
    D. Congress of Industrial Organizations ... organized skilled workers into craft unions.
    E. United Mine Workers ... embraced the leadership and tactics of John L. Lewis.

39. Members of the Beat Generation are best characterized as
    A. African American civil rights workers like John Lewis who participated in the Freedom Rides
    B. hippies like Bob Dylan who wrote counterculture protest songs
    C. Dixiecrats like Strom Thurmond who walked out of the 1948 Democratic convention
    D. writers like Jack Kerouac who rejected America's mindless conformity during the 1950s
    E. consumer advocates like Ralph Nader who called attention to faulty automobiles

40. Geraldine Ferraro was the
    A. founder of the National Organization of Women (NOW)
    B. primary author of *Silent Spring*
    C. leading opponent of the Equal Rights Amendment (ERA)
    D. first woman appointed to the Supreme Court
    E. first woman vice-presidential candidate of a major party

41. The Battle of Saratoga was important because it convinced
    A. Great Britain to revoke the Coercive Acts
    B. Great Britain to offer the colonists representatives in Parliament
    C. France to openly support the American cause
    D. George Washington to abandon New York City
    E. Lincoln to issue the Emancipation Proclamation

42. A painting of a can of Campbell's soup by Andy Warhol would be most closely associated with which of the following artistic schools?
    A. The Hudson River School
    B. The Ashcan School
    C. Cubism
    D. Abstract Expressionism
    E. Pop Art

43. Henry Clay's American system called for
   A. the gradual abolition of slavery
   B. a strict policy of neutrality in international affairs
   C. a federal system of government based upon a division of power between state and national governments
   D. internal improvements that would promote increased trade among America's different regions
   E. state banks to replace the Second Bank of the United States

44. "For we must consider that we shall be as a city upon a hill, the eyes of all people are upon us. So that if we shall deal falsely with our God in this work we shall have undertaken, and so cause Him to withdraw His present help from us, we shall be made a story and a by-word through the world."

   The statement above was made by
   A. Jonathan Edwards, preaching to a mass gathering during the Great Awakening
   B. John Winthrop, expressing his belief that the Puritan colonists had a special pact with God to build a model Christian community
   C. Lord Baltimore, defining the purpose of the Maryland colony
   D. Roger Williams, defending the excessive religiosity of the Puritans
   E. Thomas Paine, urging Americans to reject British sovereignty and create an independent nation

45. D. W. Griffith's film *The Birth of a Nation* used innovative production techniques to
   A. glamorize the rise of the Ku Klux Klan
   B. dramatize the firing on Fort Sumter.
   C. portray the Ghost Dance
   D. produce Hollywood's first "talkie"
   E. reenact the signing of the Declaration of Independence

46. "The life of the law has not been logic; it has been experience." The view expressed above is most consistent with the philosophical tenets of which of the following?
   A. Pragmatism
   B. Romanticism
   C. Republicanism
   D. Puritanism
   E. Transcendentalism

47. The primary purpose of the Taft-Harley Act of 1947 was to
   A. enable veterans to receive low-interest loans
   B. ratify President Truman's decision to integrate the armed forces
   C. limit the power of labor unions
   D. extend Marshall Plan aid to Eastern Europe
   E. increase tax rates for upper-income Americans

SAT II U.S. HISTORY EXAM: THE ESSENTIAL CONTENT

48. All of the following statements about muckrakers are true EXCEPT:
    A. They exposed unsanitary practices in the meat packing industry
    B. They exposed corruption in the settlement house movement
    C. They exposed ruthless business practices in the oil industry
    D. They exposed corruption in big city governments
    E. They exposed racial injustice in the South

49. The purpose of the Bay of Pigs invasion was to
    A. galvanize opposition to the Berlin Wall
    B. overthrow the anti-American government in Iran
    C. spark a rebellion against Fidel Castro
    D. combat political unrest in Guatemala
    E. prevent the government of South Vietnam from collapsing

50. All of the following people are correctly matched with the reform movement they led EXCEPT:
    A. Dorothea Dix ... mentally ill
    B. Ida B. Wells ... anti-lynching
    C. Horace Mann ... education
    D. Carrie Chapman Catt ... suffrage
    E. Clara Barton ... temperance

51. Anne Hutchinson is most noted for her
    A. poems about frontier life
    B. unorthodox religious views
    C. outspoken support for women's suffrage
    D. emotional First Great Awakening sermons
    E. opposition to slavery

52. All of the following statements about the Monroe Doctrine are true EXCEPT:
    A. It asserted American independence in foreign policy
    B. It warned European nations that the American continents were no longer open to colonization
    C. It expressed the belief that European monarchies are antithetical to American republican institutions
    D. It was a unilateral declaration of principles
    E. It expressed a desire for a closer alliance with Great Britain

53. The Erie Canal helped promote the growth of
    A. Charleston and Savannah
    B. Boston and Chicago
    C. Buffalo and New York City
    D. Baltimore and Philadelphia
    E. Richmond and Atlanta

54. Abraham Lincoln played a key role in all of the following EXCEPT:
   A. The passage of the Compromise of 1850
   B. The rise of the Republican Party
   C. The rejection of the Crittenden Compromise
   D. The announcement of the Emancipation Proclamation
   E. The drafting of the Thirteenth Amendment

55. Which of the following tactics was NOT used to minimize African American voting rights in the South during the late 19th and early 20th centuries?
   A. Grandfather clauses
   B. Literacy tests
   C. Poll taxes
   D. White primaries
   E. Loyalty oaths

56. What was the first war in which the United States gained overseas territory?
   A. War of 1812
   B. Mexican-American War
   C. Spanish-American War
   D. World War I
   E. Vietnam War

57. "The history of life on earth has been a history of interaction between living things and their surroundings. To a large extent, the physical form and the habits of the earth's vegetation and its animal life have been molded by the environment... The most alarming of all man's assaults upon the environment is the contamination of air, earth, and sea with dangerous and even lethal materials."
   The passage above is from
   A. *The Other America* by Michael Harrington
   B. *On the Road* by Jack Kerouac
   C. *The Organization Man* by William H. Whyte
   D. *How the Other Half Lives* by Jacob Riis
   E. *Silent Spring* by Rachel Carson

58. Which of the following events did NOT happen in 1968?
   A. The assassination of Dr. Martin Luther King Jr.
   B. The assassination of Robert F. Kennedy.
   C. The Tet Offensive.
   D. The election of Richard Nixon.
   E. The shooting of four students at Kent State.

59. Which of the following was the most important cash crop in the Chesapeake colonies during the 17th century?
   A. Cotton
   B. Indigo
   C. Sugar
   D. Tobacco
   E. Rice

60. The Adams-Onis Treaty of 1819
   A. provided for the joint occupation of the Oregon Territory by the United States and Great Britain
   B. allowed popular sovereignty to determine the status of slavery throughout the Western Hemisphere
   C. defined America's western boundary with New Spain
   D. permitted the United States to annex Texas
   E. renounced Spain's claims to Cuba and the Philippines

61. The cartoon shown above was designed to promote
   A. colonial unity and bolster the common defense against France
   B. Confederate unity and bolster the common defense against the Union
   C. Republican Party unity in the aftermath of the Dred Scott decision
   D. National unity to support the Embargo of 1807
   E. Federalist Party unity during the presidential election of 1800

62. The Trail of Tears refers to
   A. the relocation of Japanese Americans during World War II
   B. the capture of anti-Castro forces following the Bay of Pigs invasion
   C. the relocation of Native Americans to the Indian Territory in Oklahoma
   D. the cries of outrage following the massacre at Wounded Knee
   E. the trail used by the Exodusters

63. The policies of Lyndon B. Johnson differed most consistently from those of Franklin D. Roosevelt in which area?
    A. Support for the arts.
    B. Help for the elderly.
    C. Increased federal spending for social services.
    D. Government-sponsored employment programs.
    E. Civil rights legislation.

64. The most probable authors of statements I, II, and III:

I. "The talented tenth of the Negro race must be made leaders of thought and missionaries of culture among their people...The Negro race, like all other races, is going to be saved by its exceptional men."

II. "When I say fight for independence right here, I don't mean any nonviolent fight, or turn-the-other cheek fight. Those days are gone, those days are over."

III. "During the days of the Montgomery Bus Boycott, I came to see the power of nonviolence more and more. As I lived through the actual experience of protest, nonviolence became more than a useful method, it became a way of life."
    A. W.E.B Du Bois, Malcolm X, and Martin Luther King Jr.
    B. Marcus Garvey, Booker T. Washington, and Stokely Carmichael
    C. Frederick Douglass, W.E.B. Du Bois, and Marcus Garvey
    D. Martin Luther King Jr., Malcolm X, and Ida B. Wells
    E. Booker T. Washington, Stokely Carmichael, and George Wallace

65. Between 1880 and 1920, the United States drew the most immigrants from
    A. Ireland and Germany
    B. England and France
    C. Canada and Mexico
    D. Italy and Russia
    E. China and Japan

66. The House of Representatives impeached Andrew Johnson because he
    A. obstructed Radical Reconstruction
    B. worked to repeal the Black Codes
    C. opposed the Homestead Act
    D. opposed the Thirteenth Amendment
    E. proposed the Compromise of 1877

67. The Populist Party platform included a call for all of the following EXCEPT:
    A. An end to discriminatory freight rates
    B. The direct election of United States senators
    C. Legislation to raise tariffs
    D. Legislation to permit the free coinage of silver
    E. Legislation to increase the market power of farmers

68. Which president is most closely associated with the spoils system?
    A. James Monroe
    B. John Quincy Adams
    C. Andrew Jackson
    D. Abraham Lincoln
    E. William Taft

69. "This, then, is held to be the duty of the man of wealth: to consider all surplus revenues which come to him simply as trust funds, which he is called upon to administer and strictly bound as a matter of duty to administer in the manner which, in his judgment, is best calculated to produce the most beneficial results for the community—the man of wealth thus becoming the mere agent and trustee for his poorer brethren."

These sentiments reflect

A. John D. Rockefeller's theory of horizontal integration

B. Andrew Carnegie's belief in the gospel of wealth

C. Robert Owen's principles of how to form a utopian community

D. Frederick W. Taylor's theory of scientific management

E. Samuel Gompers' criticism of the robber barons

70. Marcus Garvey is remembered as an African American leader who

A. promoted the talented tenth

B. promoted black pride and black nationalism

C. advocated accommodation to white society

D. advocated nonviolent civil disobedience

E. organized a march on Washington

71. John Steinbeck's *The Grapes of Wrath*

A. was originally written as a political commentary on free silver and the plight of American farmers

B. was originally written as a social satire on the excessive materialism of American life in the 1920s

C. was originally written as a political commentary on labor strife in the 1930s

D. captured the ordeal of the Plains Indians as they lost their land to the settlers

E. captured the ordeal of the Okies as they fled the Dust Bowl

72. Inflation was a primary domestic issue for which president?

A. Franklin D. Roosevelt

B. Dwight Eisenhower

C. John F. Kennedy

D. Gerald Ford

E. Ronald Reagan

73. All of the following statements about British mercantile policies are true EXCEPT:

A. They impeded the growth of colonial manufacturing

B. They were implemented by the Navigation Acts

C. They were not rigorously enforced prior to 1763

D. They reduced colonial consumption of French and Dutch goods

E. They encouraged other European powers to establish colonies in North America

74. Which of the following was established by the Constitution to safeguard the presidency from direct popular election?
    A. The two-party system
    B. A bicameral legislature
    C. The system of checks and balances
    D. The electoral college
    E. The separation of powers

75. "This treaty must of course be laid before both Houses, because both have important functions to exercise respecting it. They, I presume, will see their duty to their country in ratifying and paying for it, so as to secure a goal which would otherwise probably be never again in their power. But I suppose they must then appeal to the nation for an additional article to the Constitution, approving and confirming an act which the nation had not previously authorized."
    This statement was made by
    A. Thomas Jefferson about the purchase of the Louisiana Territory
    B. James K. Polk about the Wilmot Proviso
    C. Franklin Pierce about the Ostend Manifesto
    D. William McKinley about the annexation of the Philippines
    E. Theodore Roosevelt about the acquisition of the Panama Canal Zone

76. Which of the following groups would have been most likely to support the use of popular sovereignty in the Kansas and Nebraska territories?
    A. Whigs
    B. Republicans
    C. Southern Democrats
    D. Free Soilers
    E. Abolitionists

77. Which of the following was most responsible for President Hoover's defeat in the 1932 presidential election?
    A. The public's desire for a return to normalcy.
    B. The deepening economic depression.
    C. The rejection of the Republican Party by African American voters.
    D. The public's growing concern about the effectiveness of New Deal programs.
    E. The emergence of the Silent Majority as a key voting bloc.

78. The primary purpose of the Congress of Industrial Organizations (CIO) under John L. Lewis' leadership was to organize
    A. unskilled and semi-skilled factory workers in basic industries such as steel and automobiles
    B. skilled workers into craft unions
    C. all industrial and agricultural workers into "one big union"
    D. students and workers into a Social-Democratic labor party
    E. migrant farm workers into a union of agricultural workers

79. The purpose of the Dawes Severalty Act of 1887 was to
    A. force Native Americans to give up tribal lands and become self-sufficient farmers
    B. concentrate Native Americans on compact reservations
    C. exclude all Chinese immigrants from coming to the United States
    D. curb the power of labor unions
    E. create a new Civil Service Commission

80. Which of the following was NOT true about Shays' Rebellion?
    A. The farmers demanded an end to imprisonment for debtors.
    B. The farmers demanded an increased circulation of paper money.
    C. The farmers demanded that the government of Massachusetts be overthrown.
    D. The farmers demanded an end to farm foreclosures.
    E. The farmers demanded an end to high taxes.

81. "I hear the whistle. I must hurry. It is time to go into the shop. I change my clothes and get ready to work. The starting whistle blows."
    This excerpt from a corporate brochure distributed to workers best illustrates which of the following approaches to work?
    A. Social Darwinism
    B. Social Gospel
    C. Gospel of Wealth
    D. Taylorism
    E. Progressivism

82. Frederick Jackson Turner was the first historian to
    A. analyze the effects of the frontier on the American character
    B. analyze the impact of immigration on nativist political movements
    C. analyze the contributions of third-party movements
    D. compare and contrast the goals and methods of the Populists and the Progressives
    E. compare and contrast the New Deal and Great Society programs

83. Which of the following is a correct statement about English indentured servants?
    A. They helped suppress the Pueblo Revolt.
    B. They instigated the Stono Rebellion.
    C. They were the primary source of agricultural labor in Virginia and Maryland before 1675.
    D. They greatly outnumbered African slaves in every Southern colony by 1776.
    E. They supported Roger Williams and other Massachusetts Bay dissidents.

84. Which of the following statements best describes the primary goal of the Social Gospel movement?
   A. To enact legislation restricting the flow of immigrants from Southern and Eastern Europe.
   B. To enact legislation promoting the civil rights of African Americans living in the South.
   C. To support the annexation of the Philippines.
   D. To commit Protestant churches to accept responsibility for helping the poor.
   E. To support a constitutional amendment calling for the direct election of United States senators.

85. The Republican Party emerged as a national political force following the
   A. rejection of the Wilmot Proviso
   B. discovery of gold in California
   C. passage of the Compromise of 1850
   D. publication of *Uncle Tom's Cabin*
   E. passage of the Kansas-Nebraska Act

86. Bacon's Rebellion in 1676 illustrates the tension between
   A. Federalists and Anti-Federalists
   B. New England and the Chesapeake colonies
   C. Puritans and religious dissidents
   D. former indentured servants and the Tidewater gentry
   E. Massachusetts farmers and their creditors

87. Which of the following is true of the Missouri Compromise?
   A. It opened most of the Louisiana Territory to slavery.
   B. It accepted the principle of popular sovereignty.
   C. It inflamed the political crisis over slavery.
   D. It failed to maintain the balance between free and slave states in the Senate.
   E. It provided for the admission of Missouri as a slave state and Maine as a free state.

88. The Northwest Ordinance of 1787
   A. provided free land for settlers in the Northwest Territory
   B. called for a convention to revise the Articles of Confederation
   C. influenced Jefferson's theory of natural rights
   D. banned slavery from the Northwest Territory
   E. granted Great Britain temporary control over a number of frontier forts

89. The Freedom Rides of 1962, the Birmingham demonstration of 1963, and the Mississippi Freedom Summer of 1964 were all key events in the
   A. counterculture
   B. war on poverty
   C. civil rights movement
   D. emergence of the silent majority
   E. women's rights movement

90. Which of the following issues dominated national politics during the period from 1824 to 1836?
   A. The construction of transcontinental railroads.
   B. The enactment of high protective tariffs.
   C. The annexation of Texas.
   D. The use of popular sovereignty in the Western territories.
   E. The spread of utopian communities.

ANSWERS

1. D	24. E	47. C	70. B
2. C	25. B	48. B	71. E
3. A	26. A	49. C	72. D
4. B	27. D	50. E	73. E
5. E	28. C	51. B	74. D
6. D	29. E	52. E	75. A
7. D	30. E	53. C	76. C
8. A	31. B	54. A	77. B
9. B	32. E	55. E	78. A
10. E	33. B	56. C	79. A
11. C	34. B	57. E	80. C
12. D	35. A	58. E	81. D
13. B	36. C	59. D	82. A
14. D	37. C	60. C	83. C
15. D	38. D	61. A	84. D
16. A	39. D	62. C	85. E
17. B	40. E	63. E	86. D
18. A	41. C	64. A	87. E
19. E	42. E	65. D	88. D
20. D	43. D	66. A	89. C
21. E	44. B	67. C	90. B
22. D	45. A	68. C	
23. D	46. A	69. B	

Made in the USA
Middletown, DE
24 February 2018